Pumps

Contributors

E. Elwin Arasmith
  Terra West

Robert H. Fuller
  Robert H. Fuller & Assoc. Inc.

Richard M. Holl
  Industrial Training Consultant

John H. O'Neill

Editor

Linda Warner

Graphic Design

Robert A. Ravelo

Schoolcraft
PUBLISHING

A division of
Telemedia, Inc.

Table of Contents

Chapter One

Use of Pumps

The Development of Pumps

1.01   One of the earliest pumping devices in recorded history is the *Archimedean screw,* developed in Greece in the third century BC. The device is simply a broad-threaded screw encased in a cylinder or in an open trough. In ancient times, an operator at the top of the screw turned a hand crank that turned the screw, raising the water higher with each revolution. The screw was used for irrigation purposes and for raising water from mines, ship holds, and other confined spaces. These devices are still used today in water treatment plants. Figure 1-1 shows several

Fig. 1-1. Archimedean screws

Fig. 1-2. Noria with free-swinging buckets

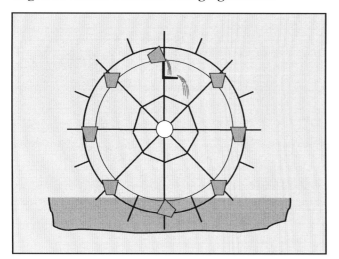

screws in use at the Indianapolis Advanced Water Treatment facility.

1.02   The first pumping device employing neither human nor animal power was probably developed in China. The device, called a *noria,* consisted of many open-ended bamboo tubes attached around the edge of a large wheel. As the current of a river caused the wheel to turn, each tube dipped into the river and carried a small amount of water up to a channel located near the top of the wheel. Here the tubes spilled their water and returned to the river.

1.03   An early modification of the noria is illustrated in Fig. 1-2. This device employed free-swinging buckets attached to a wheel by pins. Their free-swinging nature prevented the buckets from dumping their contents before reaching the top of the wheel. When a bucket reached the top of the wheel it struck a bar that caused it to tip and empty its contents into a trough. The maximum lift of the noria was limited by the diameter of the wheel, usually 30 to 40 ft. Use of the noria was also limited by the fact that it could not operate in wells or other confined spaces.

1.04   Ancient Egyptians are credited with inventing a device for pumping water from deep wells. It consisted of a series of buckets or pots mounted on an endless chain rather than on a wheel. The chain was driven by humans or by oxen. This device is shown in Fig. 1-3. Simple pumping machines like these are still used today for irrigation in areas of the Far East.

Fig. 1-3. Chain of pots

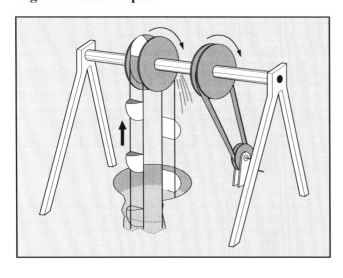

1.05   Figure 1-4 is a drawing of an early positive-displacement pump. A *positive-displacement pump* discharges a known quantity of fluid during a piston movement through a stroke distance. This pump remained substantially unchanged until the beginning of the Industrial Revolution in late eighteenth-century England. At this time, a steam-powered, positive-displacement pump was developed. The centrifugal pump first appeared in the mid 1800s.

1.06   In industry today, pumps are second only to electric motors as the most commonly used type of equipment. Pumps allow fluids to be moved through pipes, raised to higher elevations, or stored under pressure. Some pumps are even used to move cement and other solids. The remainder of this chapter describes several applications of modern pumps in typical pumping systems, perhaps like those used in your plant.

Pumping Systems

1.07   Nearly all industrial plants use pumps in some way. The pumping of materials can create many challenges for both operating and maintenance personnel.

Fig. 1-4. Early positive-displacement pump

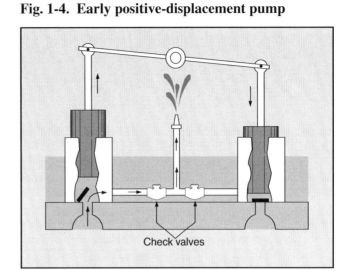

Check valves

1.08   Problems in pumping systems can usually be traced to the pump itself, but can also be the result of improper piping or poor selection of valves or accessories. Extending or modifying an existing piping system is a project often assigned to the maintenance department.

1.09   Some pumping systems described in this chapter probably resemble those located in your plant. Even if the systems are different, the basic principles and operating procedures will be similar. The main objective of this chapter is to describe various pump and piping systems used in industrial plants.

Water Pumping Systems

1.10   Water systems are the most common pumping systems in a plant. Although municipal water systems supply water to most plants, some plants have their own wells or other supply sources. Some plants have special requirements, such as water under high pressure, chemically treated water, or water circulation within the plant.

1.11   A typical direct water supply system is shown in Fig. 1-5, on the following page. A pump withdraws water from a reservoir, lake, well, or other supply source. A centrifugal pump is usually used for this purpose. The water is then conditioned to make it usable for drinking and other purposes. Conditioning can include such processes as softening, filtering, settling, and chemical treatment. From the conditioning tanks, pumps raise the water to an elevated storage tank. After leaving the storage tank, a piping system distributes the water to the required points within the plant.

Fig. 1-5. Typical water supply system

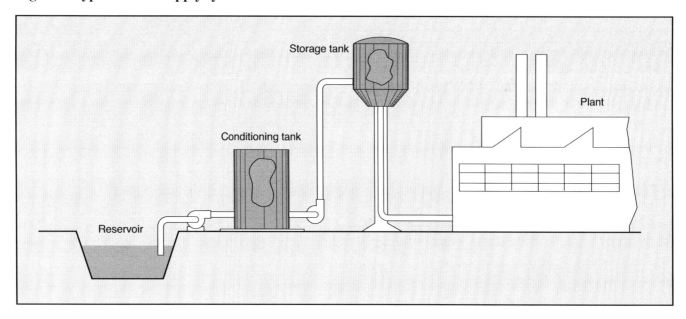

1.12   Plants with special water treatment requirements often use modifications of the system just described. For example, water might be treated for use with a specific piece of equipment and supplied directly to the equipment without passing through a conditioning tank. Boiler feedwater systems commonly use an arrangement similar to this. The necessary chemicals are added to the water in specific amounts just before the water is pumped into the boiler. The chemicals are often mixed in advance and held in a small storage tank until they are added to the boiler feedwater system.

1.13   Industrial plants use many types of chemical additive systems that resemble the boiler feedwater system. You might have one or more of these in your plant. The feed pumps used in additive systems are often metering pumps. If metering pumps are not used, some other means of control must be provided to regulate the flow of the chemicals or other additives.

1.14   The pumping systems just described are relatively easy to understand. Several application problems exist, however, even in these simple systems. One, of course, is choosing the right kind of pump. In addition, pump pressures must be sufficient to overcome changes in the elevation of the water and pressure in the piping. Also, the pumps and piping must be constructed of materials that are capable of handling the water and chemical solutions without becoming damaged or corroded.

1.15   Another pumping system common to most industrial plants is the hot water distribution system. A hot water distribution system can be either a *dead-end system* or a *recirculating system*. Both types are shown in Fig. 1-6. The type used in a particular case depends upon plant requirements. If a large amount of hot water is required in one specific area, a dead-end system is probably the best choice. If hot water is required throughout the plant, a recirculating system might be more economical. In a recirculating system, unused hot water can be reheated along with a small amount of incoming cool water. This type of system not only eliminates the need to heat all cool water, but also saves heat that would be wasted as water cooled in the lines.

Chemical Pumping Systems

1.16   Chemical pumping systems are unique in their design. Most of their special construction and design requirements are necessary because of the nature of the materials they handle. The chemicals handled in one area of a plant might not require the use of special corrosion-resistant materials. The corrosion-resistant material used in one pump for one chemical might not be suitable for use with another chemical. In such cases, two separate systems must be used. Piping requirements also vary with the material being pumped.

1.17   Another factor to be considered when selecting a pump is the flow resistance of the chemical. If the chemical is a slurry, it might be necessary to use a positive-displacement pump rather than a centrifugal pump. The viscosity (resistance to flow) of the chemical determines the kind of pump selected. Applications in which chemicals must be metered or pumped under high pressure require high-powered positive-displacement pumps.

Fig. 1-6. Hot water distribution systems

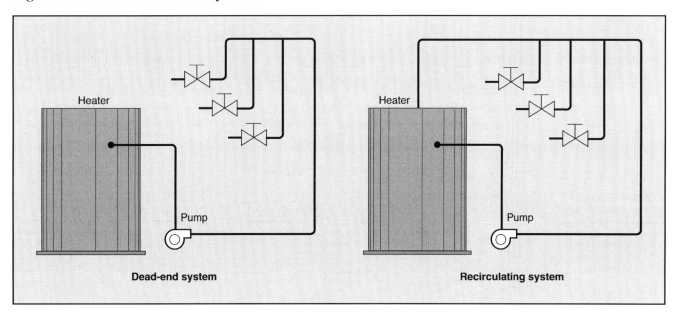

1.18   Chemical pumping systems often require special gaskets, seals, and packing materials. The materials used to manufacture seals for pumps having a corrosion-resistant casing are not the same as those used for pumps without this casing. As a result, you must give special consideration to the seals used. They must not only withstand the corroding action of the chemical, but must also be compatible with the corrosion-resistant materials used in the pump.

1.19   Chemical handling, like water distribution, can involve a wide variety of pump and piping arrangements. The plant layout and the requirements of the particular application determine the arrangement. For example, one chemical pumping system might be an in-plant operation limited to only a small area, as shown in Fig. 1-7. In this case, dry chemicals are stored in elevated bins on the second floor of the plant. Feed spouts or chutes extend down to the first-floor mixing area. On the first floor, several dry chemicals are blended in a mixing tank, then combined with water or other liquids to produce the desired chemical solution. The chemical solution is then pumped to a filling machine, which dispenses it into bottles, cans, drums, or other containers. Similar operations take place in most bottling plants.

1.20   In another type of operation, a plant might manufacture chemicals in a process similar to the one just described. But instead of filling containers, pumps move the chemicals into large storage tanks that are located either outside the building or within. The fluid is later pumped from the storage tanks to rail cars or trucks for shipment to other plants, where it is processed further. Or, the chemicals might be pumped from one building to another within the plant complex for further processing to

Fig. 1-7. Chemical pumping system

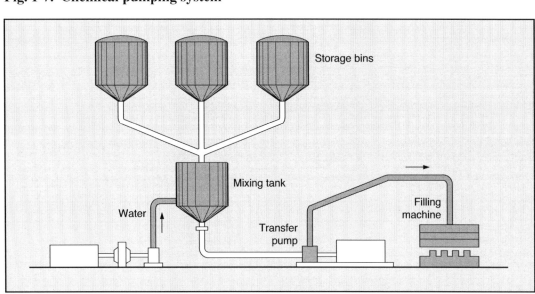

make a different product. A good example of this type of operation is an oil refinery.

1.21   Frequently, chemical products must remain within a specific temperature range while they are being pumped from one location to another. In such cases, the piping systems carrying the chemicals must be fully insulated to maintain the proper temperature. Insulated piping systems are also necessary for piping hot water or steam within an industrial plant complex.

Waste Pumping Systems

1.22   Waste pumping systems, like chemical pumping systems, have a variety of applications. For example, one system might handle roof runoff water, another sewage wastes, and yet another chemical wastes and radioactive wastewater. Generally, centrifugal pumps are used to pump wastewater in a plant. The low-head pumping requirements and the pump's ability to pass small solid particles make the centrifugal pump well suited to these applications. Usually, the waste is piped directly to the pump. Often, the pump is completely submerged in the liquid it is pumping, like the sump pump shown in Fig. 1-8.

1.23   If the pump is handling corrosive waste, the pump impeller, housing, shaft, and supporting structure must be made of corrosion-resistant materials. If the pump is handling runoff water or other noncorrosive waste, it can be made of cast iron, bronze, or brass and will usually have good service life. When sump pumps are used, intake screens must be installed to keep large particles from reaching the pump impeller.

1.24   When pumping radioactive or chemical wastes, pumps are often connected to independent collection and discharge systems. Chemical wastes might be pumped through one system, while floor drainage and other wastewater are conveyed through a separate system to a second sump, as shown in Fig. 1-9, on the following page. Since the chemical pump is located outside of the sump, only the internal parts of the pump come into contact with the waste. Therefore, only the internal pump parts must be able to withstand the action of the chemical. The pump discharges the waste into an elevated waste storage tank for temporary storage. From this point, the waste is picked up by truck, rail car, or other means and is disposed of

Fig. 1-8. Waste pumping arrangement

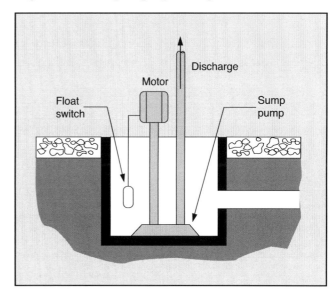

Fig. 1-9. Separate waste systems

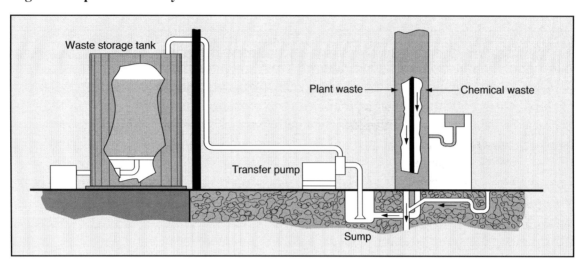

where the waste chemicals will not harm or pollute any existing water sources or disposal facilities.

1.25   The pulp, paper, and canning industries offer many examples of special waste disposal facilities. These industries produce large amounts of wastewater in a short time. Because of the nature of the wastewater, it cannot be discharged into municipal sewage systems, rivers, or lakes. In these cases, companies usually have treatment plants installed on company property. The treatment plants process and purify the water before it is discharged into municipal sewage facilities or bodies of water.

1.26   Another example of chemical waste treatment is the paint spray booth shown in Fig. 1-10. Air passes through the painting area into the water curtains of the spray booth. As the air and paint pass through several curtains of water, the water collects the paint pigments. The water returns to the reservoir, where the paint pigments settle to the bottom. Water from the reservoir is supplied to the spray header pipe by a recirculating pump that is mounted outside of the spray booth. The paint spray booth is an example of a closed circulation system operating in a small area.

1.27   Because spray booths require large quantities of water, it is impractical to supply fresh, unused water continuously. By using a recirculating system, far less water is used. The water is changed at regular intervals, and the paint pigments are collected from the bottom of the reservoir.

High-Viscosity Material Pumping Systems

1.28   *Viscosity* is the property of a material that resists any flow-producing force. High-viscosity materials include syrups, oils, and light cement slurries. The degree of viscosity of materials varies from plant to plant. The materials covered in this section are fairly thick but still flow when pumped.

1.29   Positive-displacement pumps (both rotary and reciprocating) are generally used for pumping high-viscosity materials. The nature of the material being pumped frequently limits the area of system operation. The length of pipe runs is limited by the distance the material can be pumped without using booster pumps, which add to energy consumption. In some cases, the fluid being pumped can be heated to lower its viscosity and make it easier to pump. Pipe runs are then insulated to maintain the elevated temperature of the fluid.

Fig. 1-10. Typical paint spray booth

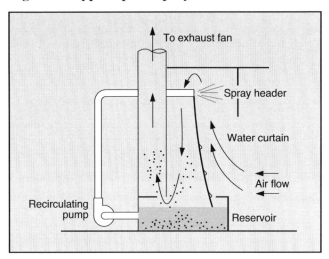

1.30   Paint is another example of a high-viscosity fluid. Piston pumps are usually used to handle paint. Often the paint is pumped directly from the drum, through a system of filters and strainers, to the spray gun, as shown in Fig. 1-11.

1.31   Some paint systems do not pump from a drum, but rather use compressed air to force the paint from a pressurized storage tank. This arrangement is also shown in Fig. 1-11. The paint moves through a heater and then to the spray gun. When heaters are used, they usually contain small, air-driven, circulating gear pumps to help keep the paint in motion.

Fig. 1-11. Paint spray systems

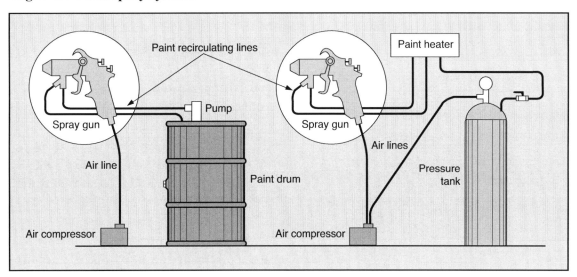

1.32   One of the problems involved with paint pumping systems is the settling of pigments as they travel through the supply lines. To avoid pigment settling, the paint must be kept in motion and must move relatively quickly.

1.33   Another problem in spray paint systems involves the abrasiveness of paint pigment. Although paint feels slippery when you rub it between your fingers, the pigment that gives paint its color is very abrasive. This abrasiveness causes wear within the pump.

1.34   Light cement slurries and glue are usually pumped with piston pumps. In these applications, heat need not be added. Because of the high water content of these materials, they flow quite easily at room temperature. Heat applied to these materials tends to set them or dry them out, causing problems within the piping system.

1.35   Because of their weight, cement slurries are usually withdrawn from a holding tank or hopper located above the pump. Cement slurries can be pumped long distances without encountering many problems. The piping through which the materials flow should be large enough to allow them to flow with a minimum of friction. An example of a cement slurry pumping operation is shown in Fig. 1-12. Notice that the receiving hopper is located above the pump.

Solids Pumping Systems

1.36   Solids pumping systems are similar in nature to high-viscosity material systems. They differ only by the characteristics of the material being pumped. Solids pumping systems handle greases, heavy mastics, cement, concrete, and similar materials. The cement slurry pumping system previously described is equally effective for pumping dry cement.

1.37   When pumping concrete, a pump must be able to pass a large quantity of stone and gravel. For this reason, pumps must be heavily constructed with large suction and discharge ports. Because of the abrasiveness of the sand in the concrete, excessive wear is frequently a problem. Repair will therefore be easier if cylinder liners and other replaceable components are used.

1.38   Mastic and grease pumping systems are usually of the dead-end or noncirculating

Fig. 1-12. Cement slurry pumping system

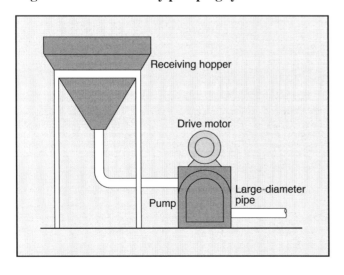

Fig. 1-13. Grease or mastic pumping systems

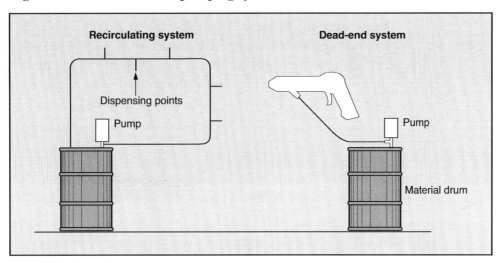

type shown at the right in Fig. 1-13. Recirculating systems are sometimes used when several stations demand large quantities throughout the day. A recirculating system is shown at the left in Fig. 1-13.

1.39   Piston pumps are most often used to handle materials like these. One common problem encountered with a piston pump, however, involves the flow at the source of supply. The pump can usually withdraw the material (grease, for example) faster than the material can flow down to the pump, as shown in Fig. 1-14. To overcome this problem, grease drums using piston pumps are usually equipped with a *follower plate,* as shown. This follower plate rides on top of the material being pumped. The use of a follower plate is also shown in Fig. 1-14.

Fig. 1-14. Use of a follower plate

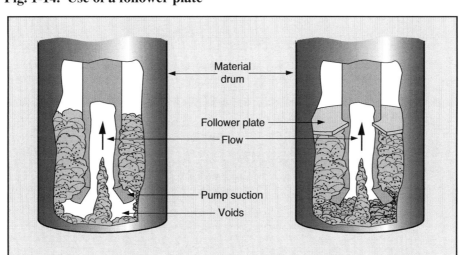

1.40   The suction of the pump draws the level of the grease or mastic down toward the bottom of the drum. The weight of the follower plate helps force the material down. The plate also prevents the formation of air pockets or voids between the pump suction and the grease surface. A rubber gasket placed around the outer edge of the plate scrapes the drum clean as it travels down and ensures that most of the grease gets to the pump.

Chapter Two

Pump Hydraulics

Pumping Terminology

2.01 A basic understanding of pump hydraulics is important for both maintenance and operating personnel. You might need to evaluate the effect that rpm or suction condition have on horsepower requirements, discharge pressure, or discharge quantity. Although you need not be able to do complex mathematics, some math background is helpful.

2.02 First, consider two classic pump installations. The first is called the *suction lift* condition. In this case, the eye of the impeller is above the fluid level, as shown in Fig. 2-1. The second is called the *suction head*, *positive suction,* or *flooded suction* condition. In this case, the eye of the impeller is below the liquid level, as shown in Fig. 2-2. Pump conditions

Fig. 2-1. Pump operating with suction lift

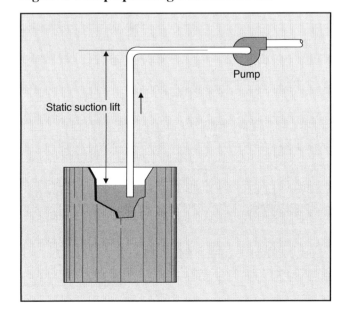

Fig. 2-2. Pump operating with suction head

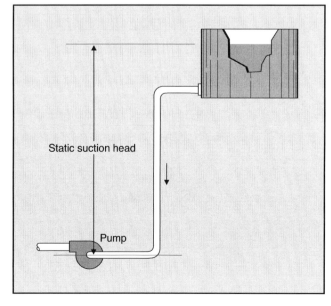

are also referred to as *static* (when the pump is not running) and *dynamic* (when the pump is running).

2.03   A column of liquid in a vertical pipe exerts a certain pressure on the horizontal surface at the bottom of the pipe. This pressure can be expressed in units of pressure (psi, for example) or as vertical distance (feet of head). Feet of head can be determined from pressure as follows:

$$\frac{\text{psi} \times 2.31}{\text{specific gravity}} = \text{ft of head}$$

2.04   The power required to drive a pump is based on its capacity and on the *head* against which it operates. The *total head* against which a pump operates takes into account several elements, including suction and discharge conditions. These elements are covered in the paragraphs that follow. We will examine the suction lift condition first.

2.05   With the pump shut off, the physical difference in elevation between the suction liquid level and the discharge liquid level is called *static head* or *elevation head*. This static head can be broken down into two components, as shown in Fig. 2-3A. The vertical distance from the suction liquid level to the eye of the impeller is called the *static suction*

Fig. 2-3. Illustration of static head

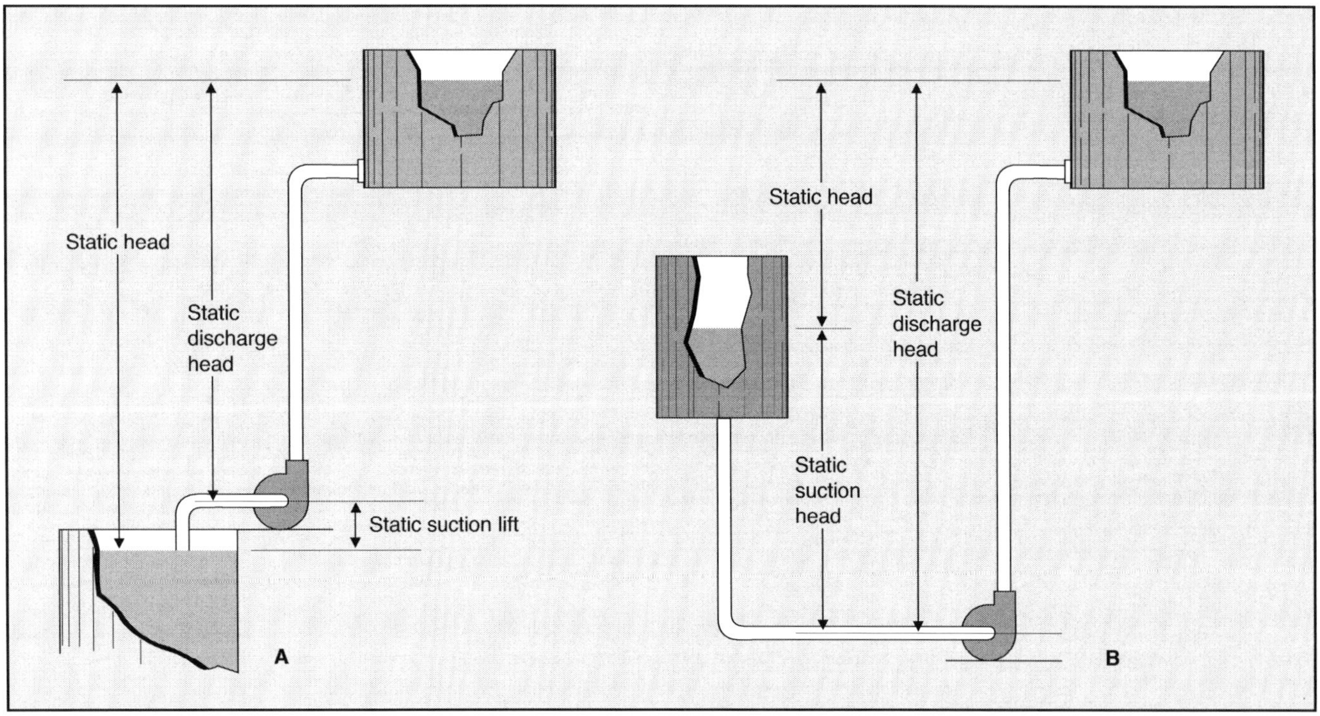

lift. The vertical distance between the eye of the impeller and the discharge liquid level is called *static discharge head.*

2.06   Energy is needed not only to move the liquid being pumped, energy is also needed to overcome friction due to pipe wall roughness and pipe fittings. Standard tables of formulas are used to calculate these factors. The total is called *head loss* or friction head. Head loss is usually expressed in feet. It represents an additional effective distance that the pump must move the liquid. The normal method of looking at head loss is to refer to the *suction head loss* and *discharge head loss* as separate components. In calculating head loss, these two must be considered individually. From an operation standpoint, you can consider head loss a single item.

2.07   There is one other factor related to total head—the amount of energy that it takes to accelerate the liquid. This energy input is referred to as *velocity head.* Velocity head is directly related to the velocity of the pumped liquid. That is, if the liquid in a pipe were moving at 3 ft/s and you wanted to increase its speed to 5 ft/s, additional energy would be required. Velocity head is equal to the distance the liquid would have to fall to acquire the same velocity. It is expressed mathematically as:

$$\frac{V^2}{2g} = \text{ft}$$

where V = velocity, in ft/s

g = acceleration due to gravity, which is 32.2 ft/s^2.

In most pump installations, velocity head is 1 ft or less. From an engineering standpoint, however, it must be calculated.

2.08   If suction and discharge pipes are the same size in a particular application, the velocity head need be calculated only once. In most installations, however, the discharge pipe is smaller in diameter than the suction pipe, even though the same amount of liquid flows through both pipes. For this reason, the velocity of liquid in the discharge pipe is higher than the velocity in the suction pipe. The result is an increase in discharge velocity head.

2.09   The sum of the total static head, head loss, and velocity head is called *total dynamic head* (TDH) or simply *total head.* Total head can be divided into dynamic suction lift and dynamic discharge head.

2.10   When dealing with a suction head condition, as shown in Fig. 2-3B, the calculations are the same as in the suction lift condition. There is a change in terminology, however, on the suction side of the pump. The distance between the eye of the impeller and the suction liquid level is called *static suction head* (instead of static suction lift). The dynamic terms are also changed to indicate this changed condition.

Calculating Total Head

2.11   When designing a pumping installation, an engineer would calculate *theoretical* total head by using formulas and tables for head loss. These calculations, which were briefly described in previous paragraphs, are based on an assumed flow.

2.12   Once a pump is installed, however, the actual total head can be calculated. If you know this value and the diameter of the impeller and have a pump curve, you can calculate the theoretical flow from a pump. You can then compare this value to a pump's actual flow to determine overall pump conditions. There are three typical conditions for which you can calculate actual total head—suction head condition, suction lift condition, and submersible and lineshaft turbines. In each of these examples, the liquid being pumped is water. For other liquids, you will have to find the specific gravity of the liquid on a table of specific gravities.

2.13   **Suction head.** In this arrangement, you must place a pressure gauge on each side of the pump and record the two pressures while the pump is operating. This arrangement is shown in Fig. 2-4. Under these conditions, the formula for total head is:

$$\frac{(Pd - Ps) \times 2.31 \text{ ft/psi}}{\text{specific gravity}} = \text{total head (ft)}$$

Fig. 2-4. Calculating total head–suction head condition

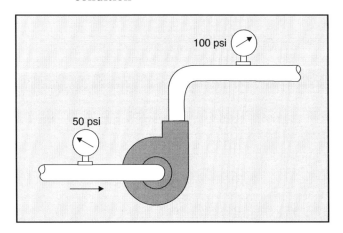

Fig. 2-5. Calculating total head–suction lift condition

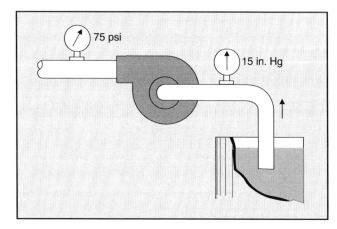

where P_d = discharge pressure

P_s = suction pressure.

From the example in Fig. 2-4, this is:

$$\frac{(100 \text{ psi } - 50 \text{ psi}) \times 2.31 \text{ ft/psi}}{1} = 115.5 \text{ ft}$$

2.14 **Suction lift.** Under suction lift conditions, you will need a vacuum gauge on the suction line and a pressure gauge on the discharge line, as shown in Fig. 2-5.

The formula for calculating total head is as follows:

$$\frac{(Pd \times 2.31 \text{ ft/psi}) + (\text{in. Hg} \times 1.13 \text{ ft/in.})}{\text{specific gravity}}$$

$$= \text{ total head (ft).}$$

The 1.13 ft/in. factor converts the vacuum reading to a height in feet. This should be the same value you would obtain if a physical measurement were made between the liquid level and the eye of the impeller. For our example, the calculations are as follows:

$$\frac{(75 \text{ psi} \times 2.31 \text{ ft/psi}) + (15 \text{ in. Hg} \times 1.13 \text{ ft/in.})}{1}$$

$$= 190.2 \text{ ft.}$$

2.15 **Submersible pumps and lineshaft turbines.** Under these conditions, the formula is as follows:

$$\frac{(Pd \times 2.31 \text{ ft/psi}) + \text{ lift}}{\text{specific gravity}} = \text{total head (ft)}$$

For the example shown in Fig. 2-6, on the following page, the calculations are as follows:

$$\frac{125 \text{ psi} \times 2.31 \text{ ft/psi} + 58 \text{ ft}}{1} = \text{total head}$$

$$288.75 \text{ ft} + 58 \text{ ft } = 346.75.$$

Fig. 2-6. Calculating total head–submersible pump

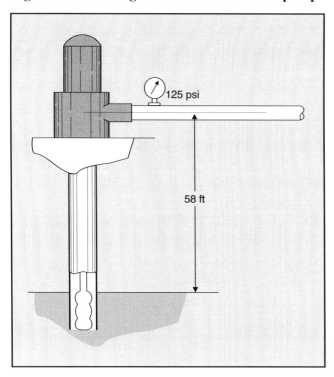

The accuracy of these calculations depends on the accuracy of the gauges and measurements.

2.16　This type of calculation does not give you the maximum possible total head but the actual total head for the existing conditions. These calculations are a reflection of velocity head, head loss, and static elevation heads. Besides being useful in comparing pump performances, the calculations for total head can be used to determine horsepower requirements.

Horsepower Calculations

2.17　In a typical pump installation, there are three related horsepower calculations that you should understand (see Fig. 2-7). The hydraulic power that the pump transfers to the pumped liquid is called *liquid horsepower.* The horsepower input to the pump is referred to as *brake horsepower.* This value is greater than the liquid horsepower by a factor representing the efficiency of the pump. The *electrical horsepower* required to run the motor (to deliver the required brake horsepower) is larger than the brake horsepower by a factor representing the efficiency of the motor.

2.18　The calculations must start with the liquid horsepower requirement. The amount of energy required to raise liquid a given amount is measured in foot-pounds (ft-lb). One ft-lb of energy is the amount of energy needed to raise 1 lb of liquid 1 ft.

Fig. 2-7. Three kinds of horsepower

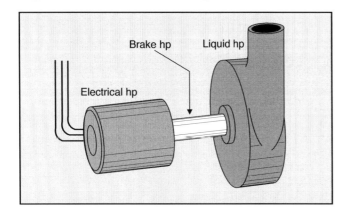

2.19　The energy required to move the liquid is affected by total head. The weight of the liquid moved is a reflection of the flow converted to weight in pounds. For example, moving 100 gallons of water is the same as moving 834 lb of water, since one gallon of water weighs 8.34 lb.

2.20　If you were to move 100 gallons of water through 200 ft of total head, the energy required would be:

$$200 \text{ ft} \times (100 \text{ gal} \times 8.34 \text{ lb/gal}) = 166{,}800 \text{ ft-lb.}$$

If you were to move this 100 gallons in 1 minute, the energy consumption would be 166,800 ft-lb/min.

2.21   Since the common method of expressing energy consumption is horsepower, you need to convert ft-lb/min to horsepower. The conversion is as follows:

1 hp = 33,000 ft-lb/min.

Therefore, energy consumption is:

$$\frac{166,800 \text{ ft - lb/min}}{33,000 \text{ ft - lb/min/hp}} = 5 \text{ hp}$$

2.22   This 5 hp is liquid horsepower, the true energy transferred from the pump to the liquid. Now that all of these conversions have been made, you can write a new equation for the calculation of liquid horsepower.

$$\text{Liquid hp} = \frac{\text{total head(ft)} \times \text{flow(gpm)} \times 8.34 \text{ lb/gal}}{33,000 \text{ ft - lb/min/hp}}$$

2.23   To compute brake horsepower, you need to know the efficiency of the pump. For example, assume that the pump you were using in the previous example is 75% efficient. The brake horsepower is calculated as follows:

$$\text{Brake hp} = \frac{\text{liquid hp}}{\% \text{ effciency of pump}} = \frac{5 \text{ hp}}{0.75} = 6.67$$

This is the energy input required by the pump. It is also the energy output required of the motor.

2.24   The computation of electrical horsepower is based on brake horsepower and motor efficiency and is determined as follows:

$$\text{Electrical hp} = \frac{\text{brake hp}}{\% \text{ efficiency of motor}}$$

If you assume for the above condition that the motor is 90% efficient, then the electrical horsepower is as follows:

$$\text{Electrical hp} = \frac{6.67 \text{ brake hp}}{0.90} = 7.4 \text{ electrical hp}$$

2.25   It took 5 hp to get the job done, but you had to purchase 7.4 hp. The 2.4 hp increase is lost to heat in the motor and pump. In reality, this is not considered to be an exceptionally large loss.

Total Energy vs Available NPSH

2.26   When a pump is in a suction lift condition, the only energy available is the atmospheric pressure—14.7 psia, or approximately 34 ft of water. Several factors combine to reduce the effect of this atmospheric pressure. The amount of energy remaining after the energy consumption factors have been satisfied is called *available net positive suction head (NPSH)*.

2.27   When liquid in a column is placed under a vacuum, a portion of the liquid will evaporate and form vapor, which will reduce available energy. This vapor pressure increases with an increase in liquid temperature.

2.28   Energy is required to overcome the distance that the liquid must be lifted, to make the liquid move (velocity head), and to overcome the friction of the pipe and fittings (friction head or head loss). The available NPSH, then, is the atmospheric pressure minus vapor pressure, static suction lift, and head loss due to friction. The pressure in psia at the eye of the impeller is the NPSH minus velocity head. Figure 2-8 illustrates this concept.

Fig. 2-8. Available NPSH–suction lift condition

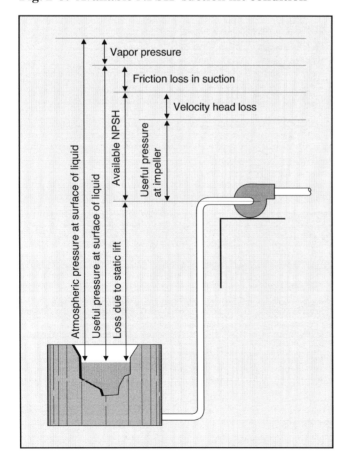

2.29   The largest single contributing factor to the reduction of pressure at the impeller is the lift itself. Even small changes in the height of liquid below the eye of the impeller will have a drastic effect upon the amount of liquid pumped.

2.30   From an absolute pressure standpoint, the liquid must enter the impeller eye under positive pressure in order for the pump to function. The higher the positive pressure, the greater the pump discharge.

2.31   When the eye of the impeller of a pump is below the level of the liquid source that supplies the suction (suction head condition), the available NPSH is the sum of atmospheric pressure and the height of the liquid above the eye of the impeller minus vapor pressure and minus friction loss.

Available NPSH vs Required NPSH

2.32   The NPSH discussion so far has been aimed at determining the available NPSH. Most pump curves will give a required NPSH as a part of the curve. It is necessary that the available NPSH be at least as large as the required NPSH in order for the curves to be valid.

2.33   Under a suction lift condition, the NPSH should be calculated. However, for suction head conditions, the usual practice is to measure the height of liquid above the eye of the impeller. If this distance meets or exceeds the required NPSH, the pump conditions, as defined by the curve, can be used. The assumption here is that atmospheric pressure will be sufficient to overcome losses due to friction, velocity head, and vapor pressure.

Pump Performance Curves

2.34   A *pump performance curve* is a vital piece of information that can be essential to operators and maintenance personnel alike. Each combination of pump and impeller has a unique set of performance curves. Any new pump should come with installation, operation, and maintenance data and with pump curves. Files should contain curves on every pump in the plant.

2.35   Pump curves can be used to select a pump for a set condition, or they can be used to help determine the effects of changes in impeller diameter, speed, and suction lift on horsepower requirements, flow, and efficiency.

2.36   There are three basic types of curves used for centrifugal pumps—the head capacity curve, the efficiency curve, and the horsepower demand curve. Some pump curves also include a curve for NPSH. Before looking at specific curves, you must know:

- the speed of the pump

- the diameter of the pump's impeller.

2.37   Figure 2-9, on the following page, shows a typical pump curve. Notice that a series of curves depicts various impeller diameters. A series of curves also shows efficiency and another brake horsepower. At first glance, this information can appear very confusing. If you analyze each type of curve individually, however, pump performance curves are much easier to understand.

Head Capacity Curves

2.38   The head capacity curve is the most basic and useful of all the pump curves. It is a graphic display of the relationship between total head

Fig. 2-9. Typical pump curve

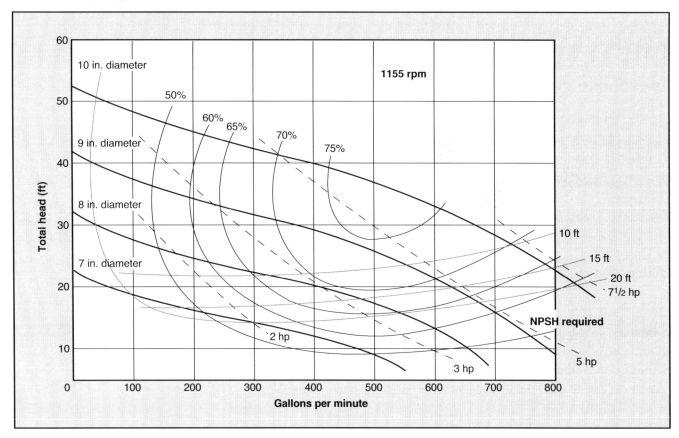

and flow conditions. Notice that the curve shown in Fig. 2-10 is for one 9 in. impeller and running at one speed—3200 rpm. Notice that for any given head, one and only one flow condition exists, and vice versa. Also, notice that for a given head, a flow can be found and for a given flow, a head can be found.

2.39   Refer to Fig. 2-10 for the following example. If a head of 300 ft is required, what flow can the pump produce? First, enter the curve from the left at 300 ft. Continue to the right in a straight line until you meet the 9 in. diameter impeller curve. Now move down in a straight line to read a flow of 230 gpm.

2.40   From the curve, you can see that the maximum total head to be expected is about 380 ft using the 9 in. impeller at 3200 rpm. Remember that this head includes suction lift (if you have one), discharge static pressure, and friction losses on both the suction and discharge side of the pump. This maximum pressure or head is reached when the pump is shut down and is referred to as *shutdown head.*

2.41   From the curve, it is easy to see how the pump responds to changes in head. If the head increases, the flow automatically

Fig. 2-10. Head capacity curve

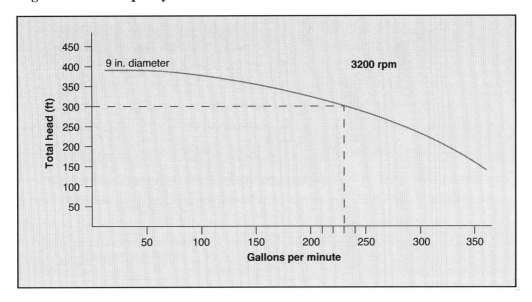

decreases. If the head decreases, the flow increases. The pressure developed by a pump is also dependent on its speed. For that reason, as speed decreases, the head capacity curve sinks straight down toward the bottom of the graph. As speed increases, the curves rise toward the top of the graph. The curve always maintains its same basic shape. The same is true for the impeller diameter. As diameter decreases, the curve sinks.

Efficiency Curves

2.42   It is important that pumps be operated so that the most amount of work can be done for a given amount of expended energy. The efficiency curve will tell you at what total head the best energy transfer will take place.

Horsepower Curves

2.43   The horsepower curve gives information on the horsepower required by the pump, not necessarily the horsepower output of the motor. For example, suppose you required 17 hp in a certain pumping situation. Motors are manufactured in 15 hp and 20 hp, but not 17 hp. Therefore, a 20 hp motor is needed. While pumping, however, the motor would be required to produce only the 17 hp. The horsepower requirement increases as flow increases. Maximum horsepower is required at maximum discharge. Minimum horsepower is required when the discharge is closed.

Curve Families

2.44   In reality, curves are usually plotted in families. For example, the bold lines in Fig. 2-9 are curves developed for various impellers that might be installed in one particular volute case. All of these curves have been plotted from an actual pump test. All tests were conducted at 1155 rpm. Notice from the impeller curves that as the diameter of an impeller is reduced, the maximum capacity is also reduced. The effect on the head, however, is much more drastic.

2.45   Rather than having a single efficiency curve, it is common to plot efficiency curves in families. These are shown by the thin lines in Fig. 2-9. Each curve connects points of common efficiency. The greatest efficiency for this particular pump is in the area of 500 gpm at 30 to 35 ft of head. At a flow of 350 gpm and a total head of 35 ft, the efficiency is 70%.

2.46   Horsepower curves are also commonly plotted in families, corresponding to available motor sizes. Figure 2-9 shows, in dashed lines, curves for four motors, from 2 to $7^1/2$ hp. For heads of less than 35 ft and flows less than 225 gpm, a 3 hp motor can be used. If, however, you have a flow of 400 gpm and a head of 30 ft, the point of intersection is about halfway between a 3 hp and a 5 hp motor. In such a case, the larger motor would be required.

2.47   There is one important curve that has not yet been discussed—the NPSH curve. This can appear as a single curve or as a family of curves. The NPSH shown by the curve is required NPSH, not available NPSH. The required NPSH influences capacity more than head. Notice that for 9 in. impellers, flows less than 550 gpm require a NPSH of 10 ft or less, while a flow of 625 gpm would require at least 15 ft of head.

2.48   The pump curve shown in Fig. 2-9 is only one type typically available from manufacturers. Some pump curves are plotted for a single impeller diameter at various speeds rather than various impeller diameters at a single speed. Both types are usually available from manufacturers.

2.49   For pumps that have more than one impeller and in which all impellers are identical, one set of curves is usually given for one impeller. Since the capacity of a pump is dependent upon the first impeller that the liquid encounters, the addition of impellers adds energy to the liquid. This additional energy results in a direct increase in head and horsepower. For example, suppose a pump operating at 1460 rpm has one impeller with a diameter of $7^1/8$ in. At a flow rate of 350 gpm, the head is 25 ft and 2 hp is required. If the pump contains two impellers, the head is increased to 50 ft and the required horsepower to 4 hp.

Pump Selection

2.50   Although it might not be your job to select a pump for a particular application, it might be useful to know some of the things that must be considered when selecting a pump. In addition to the suction lift and total dynamic head, another one of these considerations is the capacity of the pump. Normally, the capacity is given in gallons per minute or cubic feet per second. The liquid used to rate pump capacity is water.

2.51   The speed of the pump is another factor that determines the capacity and suction lift capability of a pump. The capacity of a centrifugal pump does not vary directly with the speed. You will need to use the manufacturer's capacity charts to help you determine the pump capacity at a given speed.

2.52   The altitude at which a pump operates has a definite effect on its capacity and performance. Because of the reduced amount of air pressure at the higher altitude, less suction lift is available for the pump.

2.53   The temperature of the liquid being pumped is another determining factor when selecting a pump. Liquids pumped at low temperatures will show different pump capacity than the same fluids at high temperatures. In addition to the temperature and viscosity of the liquid, the specific gravity of the material is also important. The specific gravity and temperature of the material being pumped have a direct result on the NPSH.

Chapter Three

End-Suction Centrifugal Pumps

Introduction to Centrifugal Pumps

3.01   Centrifugal pumps normally have capacities from 5 to 500 gpm and produce heads up to 250 ft. These pumps are relatively inexpensive, quiet, dependable, compact, and simple in construction. When pumping fluids that contain more than a s mall amount of vapor, however, their capacity is reduced.

3.02   Unlike positive-displacement pumps, centrifugal pumps will not continue to produce a head when operating against a closed discharge. Centrifugal pumps perform best when pumping low-viscosity fluids. Their capacity is greatly reduced when they are used to pump heavy oils and other viscous fluids.

3.03   Centrifugal pumps can be classified in several ways. They can be divided according to:

- the kind of impeller they contain

- the number of stages they have

- their axis of rotation

- the method used to drive them

- their configuration or appearance.

3.04   This course will divide centrifugal pumps by the last method, configuration or appearance. In particular, this chapter will cover a major configuration of centrifugal pump called the *end-suction pump*. These types of pumps can be further subdivided as close coupled or frame mounted, and can be mounted vertically or horizontally. The next chapter will cover vertical and regenerative turbine pumps, which are also considered centrifugal pumps.

3.05   Because end-suction centrifugal pumps are available in a great variety of styles and have many different uses, they do not always resemble each other. They all have the same operating characteristics, however.

3.06   Because of their many applications, low initial cost, and ease of maintenance, about 80% of the pumps used in industrial plants are end-suction centrifugal pumps. They are used to move water and many other fluids. These centrifugal pumps can also be adapted for pumping slurries, wood pulp and chips, and other heavy materials. When pumping these materials, however, the pumps are made of special materials and require specially constructed impellers.

3.07   You might have helped repair a centrifugal pump at some time, or maybe you have watched the job being done. You probably found that, after the piping and casing were removed, work on the internal parts of the pump was relatively simple. This chapter describes the internal parts, construction, and operation of end-suction centrifugal pumps.

Pump Operation

3.08   The operation of a centrifugal pump is based on centrifugal force. As the fluid being pumped enters the inlet or center section of the pump, the rotating action of the impeller vanes forces it to the outside of the pump casing, as shown in Fig. 3-1. Because the fluid moves faster at the outer edge of the impeller, momentum increases. As more fluid enters the pump suction, more fluid momentum is built up in the casing that encloses the impeller. This momentum forces the fluid out of the pump discharge port.

Pump Part Definitions

3.09   Figure 3-2 shows a cross section of a single-stage, end-suction centrifugal pump. Use it for reference with the following definitions of pump parts. Even if the pumps in your plant do not look exactly like the ones shown in this chapter, definitions for the various parts will be the same.

Fig. 3-1. Fluid flow in a centrifugal pump

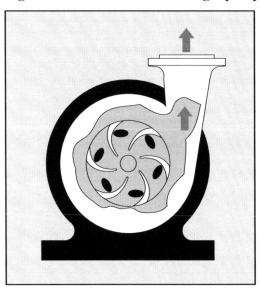

Fig. 3-2. End-suction centrifugal pump parts

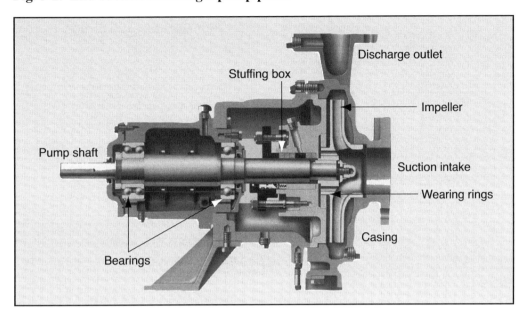

3.10   The *casing* is the enclosure surrounding the pump impeller, shaft, and stuffing box. It directs the flow of fluid into and out of the pump. Casings are usually of the *volute* or *increasing-radius* type.

3.11   Depending upon the type of motor connection used, the *pump shaft* might be part of the motor rotor, or it might be independent and coupled to the motor shaft. The shaft can be supported by its own bearings or by the motor bearings. The method used depends upon the design of the pump.

3.12   The *impeller* is the part of the pump that supplies energy to the fluid to give it velocity and momentum. The open area in the center of the impeller, called the *impeller eye*, partially determines the pump capacity. *Impeller vanes* or *blades* direct the flow of fluid within the pump. *Impeller shrouds* enclose the blades of the impeller and contain the flow of fluid in the impeller area. The portion of the impeller that mounts on the shaft is called the *impeller hub*.

3.13   The *suction intake* is the passage through which fluid enters the pump. It is normally located near the center of the casing. The diameter of the passage at this point partially determines the pump capacity. The pump discharges fluid to the piping system through the *discharge outlet*.

3.14   *Wearing rings* are not always included in the design of a pump. The main function of these replaceable rings is to maintain the small clearance between the impeller and the casing. Because even this small clearance allows some fluid leakage, abrasives in the pumped fluid can cause wear to the pump parts. Wearing rings protect the impeller and

Fig. 3-3. Double-suction centrifugal pump

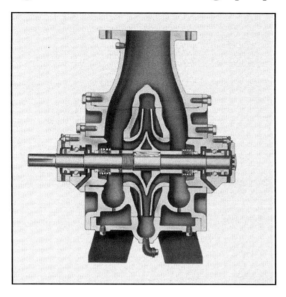

casing from damage by the abrasives. Replacing wearing rings is usually much simpler and more economical than rebuilding or replacing pump impellers or casings.

3.15   A *pump seal* seals the fluid in the pump. The seal might be either a packed *stuffing box*, which is replaceable and adjustable, or a *mechanical seal,* which consists of two polished, lubricated, mating parts running in contact with each other.

3.16   A single-stage, single-suction pump has been described here for simple illustration of pump parts. Centrifugal pumps are also made in double-suction and multistage designs. The amount of fluid to be pumped and the required pressure determine the kind of pump used.

3.17   A *double-suction pump* is shown in Fig. 3-3. Its operation is similar to that of the single-suction pump, except that fluid is drawn in on both sides of the impeller and passes out through a single discharge outlet in the casing.

3.18   *Multistage pumps* are available with either single or double suction. In a multistage pump, fluid is discharged from one impeller to the next through internal passages in the pump casing. Each stage builds up the velocity of the fluid until the desired head is reached. The additional impeller does not increase the volume output of the pump. A multistage, single-suction pump is shown in Fig. 3-4.

Pump Casing Materials

3.19   The end-suction centrifugal pumps used in industrial plants vary considerably in application. For this reason, pump casings are constructed in many different styles and types. In addition, the pump casings are made of many different materials. Cast iron, steel, and bronze are frequently used, as are many noncorrosive and abrasion-resistant alloys. A few of the casing materials used with various fluids are shown in Table 3-1.

End-Suction Casing Configurations

3.20   End-suction pumps are easy to recognize because their suction and discharge ports are normally at 90° angles to each other. They are usually

Fig. 3-4. Multistage, single-suction pump

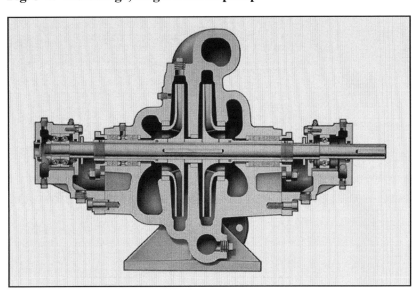

single-suction, single-stage pumps with solid casings. Two examples are shown in Fig. 3-5, on the following page.

3.21   Most end-suction pumps have a removable faceplate or cover that gives access to the impeller on the shaft. Removing the faceplate involves removal of the suction piping and possibly the discharge piping as well. Some pumps have a back pullout, which eliminates

Table 3-1. Material recommendations for corrosive substances

Liquid	Pump materials	Liquid	Pump materials	Liquid	Pump materials
Acetic acid	SS	Creosote	CI, SS	Picric acid	SS, SI
Acetone	CI, BR	Ethyl acetate	SI, SS, CI	Potassium bisulfate	BR, SS
Alcohol, ethyl (grain)	CI, BR	Ethylene chloride	SS, SI	Potassium chloride	BR, SS
Alcohol, methyl (wood)	CI, BR	Fatty acids	SS, SI	Potassium nitrate	SS, CI
Ammonia	CI, SS	Ferric chloride	R, SI, Ti	Sea water	BR, CI, SS
Ammonium hydroxide	CI, SS	Formaldehyde	SI, Ti, K	Sodium carbonate	CI, BR, SS
Ammonium nitrate	SS, SI	Formic acid	SI, K	Sodium chloride	BR, CI
Ammonium phosphate	SS, SI	Hexane	CI, SS	Sodium hydroxide	SS
Barium nitrate	CI, SS, SI	Hydrogen peroxide	SS	Sodium nitrate	SS, CI, SI
Barium sulfate	SS, SI	Isopropyl alcohol	CI	Sodium phosphate	CI, SS, BR
Benzyl acetate	SS, SI	Lye	SS	Sodium sulfide	SS, SI
Boric acid	SS, M, SI	Magnesium sulfate	SS, BR, CI	Stearic acid	SS, SI
Brine	BR, CI, M, SS	Mercuric nitrate	SS	Sulfite liquors	SS
Calcium oxide (lime)	BR, CI, SS	Methyl chloride	CI, BR, SS	Tannic acid	SS, SI
Carbolic acid (phenol)	BR, CI, SS	Naphthalene	CI, BR, SS	Titanic sulfate	SI, BR
Carbon tetrachloride	SS, M, BR	Naphthenic acid	SS	Toluene (toluol)	CI, SS, BR
Caustic soda	SS	Nitric acid	SS, SI, Ti	Trichloroethylene	CI, SS, BR
Chromic acid	Ti, SI	Oxalic acid	SS, SI, K	Xylene	SS
Copper chloride	Ti, SI	Phenol	SS, BR	Zinc phosphate	SS
Copper sulfate	SS, SI	Phosphoric acid	SI, K	Zinc sulfide	SS

Material abbreviations	BR — Bronze	M — Monel	Ti — Titanium
	CI — Cast iron	SI — Silicon iron	
	K — Karbate (impervious graphite)	SS — Stainless steel (usually 316SS)	

Fig. 3-5. End-suction centrifugal pumps

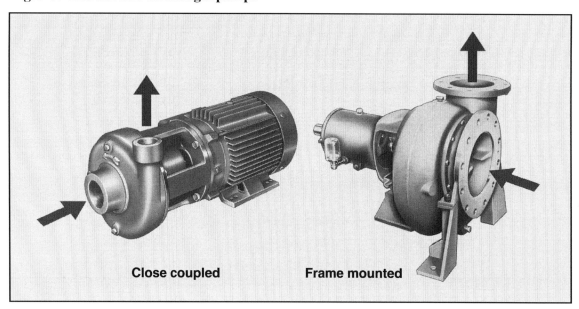

Close coupled   **Frame mounted**

the need to disconnect the piping. Both configurations are shown in Fig. 3-6.

3.22   On most end-suction pumps, it is fairly easy to change the piping connections, since the volute case can be rotated a full 360°. This feature allows for almost unlimited positioning of the pump discharge.

3.23   End-suction pumps can be either *frame mounted* or *close coupled.* Both types are shown in Fig. 3-5. In the frame-mounted pump, the pump shaft is coupled to the motor shaft. In the close-coupled pump, the impeller is mounted directly on the motor shaft. The close-coupled pump itself has no bearings. The motor bearings support the entire load of the

Fig. 3-6. Back-pullout pump

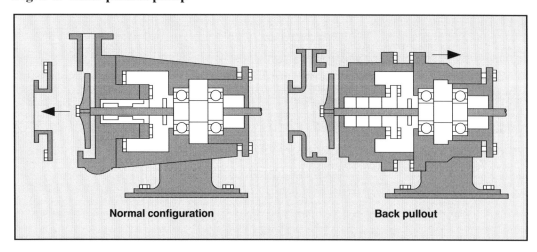

Normal configuration   **Back pullout**

impeller and motor rotor. The close-coupled pump has several advantages.

- It occupies less space.

- It eliminates vibration problems.

- It eliminates pump and motor shaft alignment problems.

3.24   End-suction pumps can be mounted either vertically or horizontally. Both of the pumps pictured in Fig. 3-5 are mounted horizontally. Figure 3-7 shows a vertically mounted, close-coupled centrifugal pump.

Split-Case Centrifugal Pumps

3.25   Some end-suction pumps have casings that are split rather than solid. *Horizontally split pumps* are easy to recognize in that their suction and discharge ports are commonly parallel but opposite each other. Fluid enters the pump perpendicular to the drive shaft, is turned 90° into the eye of the impeller, and leaves the pump perpendicular to the drive shaft. This arrangement is shown in Fig. 3-8. Notice that once the fluid enters the impeller, it moves as it would in any other end-suction pump.

3.26   The main advantage of the split-case design is that it eliminates the need to disconnect the suction and discharge piping to gain access to the pump impeller, shaft, and bearings. The upper half of the casing can be removed completely for inspection and repair purposes.

3.27   Figure 3-9, on the following page, shows a horizontally split pump. Notice that the split is made on the centerline of the shaft. The term horizontal does not refer to the position of the pump. If this pump were mounted vertically, it would still have a horizontally split casing. Horizontal split indicates the method of the split rather than the position of the pump. A horizontal split is sometimes called an axial split.

3.28   Horizontally split pumps are available with single or double suction. They are also available as multistage pumps. The pump shown

Fig. 3-7. Vertically mounted end-suction pump

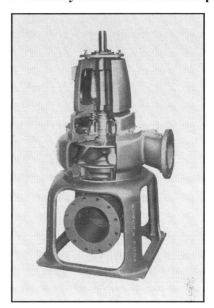

Fig. 3-8. Fluid flow in a single-stage, split-case pump

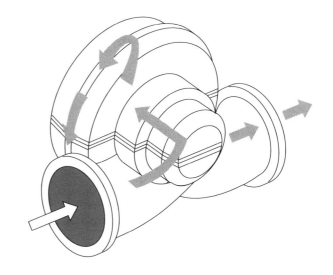

Fig. 3-9. Horizontally split pump

in Fig. 3-9 is a two-stage, single-suction pump. As is the case with other centrifugal pumps, the additional impeller of the multistage pump increases pressure, but not volume output.

3.29   Like other end-suction pumps, split-case models can be mounted vertically to save floor space. Their heavy construction gives these pumps long life. A vertically mounted split-case pump is shown in Fig. 3-10.

Fig. 3-10. Vertically mounted split-case pump

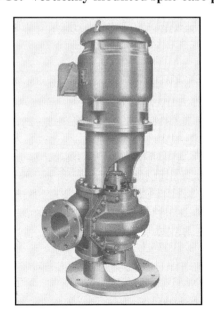

3.30   Pump casings can also be split radially. At one time, a radial split was commonly called a *vertical split*, meaning perpendicular to the centerline of the shaft. Because the term was found to be confusing, it is now usually referred to as a *radial split*.

3.31   When manufactured with a radial split, casings can be made up in segments and bolted together to form a single pump, as shown in Fig. 3-11. This feature simplifies construction and reduces casting costs involved in making a multistage pump.

Double-Volute Pumps

3.32   Although the general principles involved in the operation of end-suction pumps do not

Fig. 3-11. Radially split multistage pump

change from pump to pump, internal pump designs can vary considerably. For example, the internal fluid action in volute casings tends to produce an unbalanced radial force. To reduce this imbalance, some pumps use a *double-volute casing,* as shown in Fig. 3-12. This double volute adds a guiding vane to the fluid passage. It also splits and balances the internal radial force of the fluid, which reduces the load on the pump impeller, shaft, and bearings. Double-volute pumps are sometimes called *vane pumps.*

3.33   Double-volute guide vanes also help reduce some of the stress on the casing walls. Double-volute guide vanes are available on both solid- and split-case pumps. Guide vanes are also used on multistage pumps to balance the discharge head and guide the fluid to the suction area of the next stage.

3.34   To strengthen pump casings, many high-head pumps are manufactured with ribs around the casing exterior. These ribs are usually placed at right angles to the direction of fluid flow.

Impeller Types

3.35   The impeller is the most critical part of a pump because its size, shape, and speed

Fig. 3-12. Double-volute pump casing

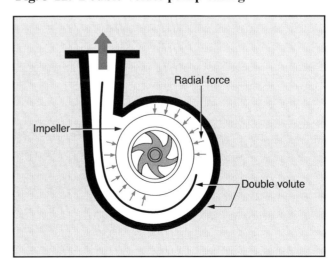

Fig. 3-13. Centrifugal pump impellers

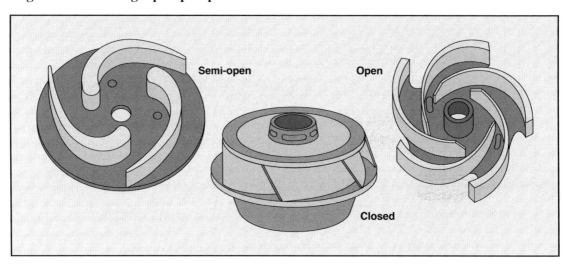

determine the pump's capacity. It is important to understand that the impeller does not cup the fluid it is pumping, but slides through the fluid and throws it. This throwing action was illustrated in Fig. 3-1.

3.36   Figure 3-13 shows three impellers. The *open impeller* has no shrouds. These impellers are used primarily for pumping fluids containing large solids.

3.37   The *semi-open impeller* has a back shroud, but no front shroud. When seen from the back, the shroud forms a complete circle. Semi-open impellers are most often used to pump fluids containing medium-sized solids. Both open and semi-open impellers are used in high-volume, low-pressure applications.

3.38   The *closed impeller* has a shroud on both front and back. Closed impellers are used to pump fluids containing few or no solids. The closed impeller is the most efficient of the three kinds in terms of energy transfer.

3.39   Impellers can have straight or curved vanes. Straight-vane impellers are commonly used in small industrial pump applications. They can be of semi-open or closed design. Curved-vane impellers (also called radial-vane impellers) are frequently used for handling fluids containing lumpy solids or heavy particles. Curved-vane impellers impart a higher velocity to the pumped fluid than do straight-vane impellers. Curved-vane impellers are available in open, semi-open, and closed designs.

3.40   A type of double-suction impeller is shown in Fig. 3-14. The double-suction type is similar to the single-suction type, except there is no backing shroud. Instead, the center of the double-suction impeller has what might be called "partial shrouds." When joined, they have a curved shape that guides the fluid from the sides of the impeller to the tips of the vanes. The vanes on each side are placed in matching positions and join to form a single vane near the outer edge of the impeller. The outer shrouds form an enclosure for the material being pumped.

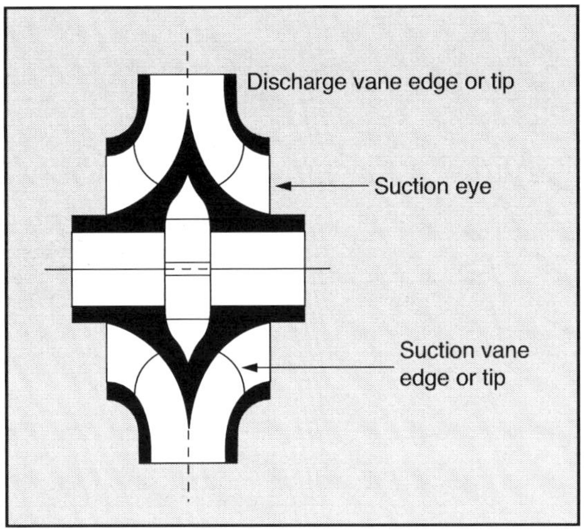

3.41   The impellers discussed so far have been only for single pumps. In multistage pumps, impeller design must be worked out carefully to avoid increasing radial and thrust loads at each stage. To offset this loading, impellers are frequently mounted back-to-back, even though they are several inches apart. Some pump impellers are equipped with small vanes on the back of the shroud to pump any fluid that gets behind the impeller. This action also helps counteract the thrust from normal impeller wear.

Fig. 3-14. Cross section of a double-suction impeller

3.42   Like pump casings, pump impellers can be made of cast iron, cast steel, fabricated steel, bronze, brass, molded rubber, fiberglass, or nearly any other material compatible with the material being pumped.

Wearing Rings

3.43   For a pump to operate correctly, there must be a physical separation between the high- and low-pressure sides. Otherwise, fluid would simply circulate from the high-pressure side to the low-pressure side and be repumped. Although the impeller separates the high and low pressure sides, a small clearance exists between the impeller and the pump casing. Even though this space is small, some fluid still passes.

3.44   When this fluid passes, some solids pass as well. These solids can cause the pump impeller and casing to wear. *Wearing rings* prevent damage to the impeller and casing. They are usually made of the same material as the impeller and casing and can be installed on the casing (both front and back) and on the impeller edges. Some typical arrangements are shown in Fig. 3-15, on the following page.

3.45   If both the casing and impeller have wearing rings, you can replace both rings without having to replace the impeller. If wearing rings are used only on the volute case, you must replace the rings and impeller at the same time.

3.46   If pumps do not have wearing rings, worn parts must be replaced or rebuilt. On some small pumps, parts replacement is fairly inexpensive.

Fig. 3-15. Wearing ring arrangements

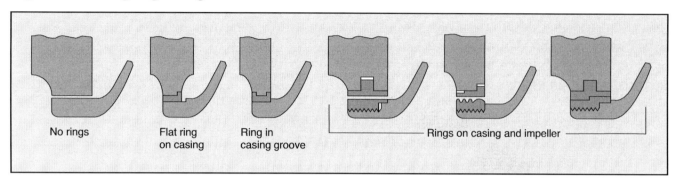

No rings   Flat ring on casing   Ring in casing groove   Rings on casing and impeller

On large pumps, however, the cost of wearing ring replacement is far less than the cost of replacing the worn parts.

Shafts, Bearings, and Sleeves

3.47　Pump shafts are normally made of stainless steel or other corrosion-resistant materials. Although corrosion-resistant materials are expensive, it is usually good practice to install a high-quality shaft despite the higher initial cost.

3.48　Shaft bearings can be of the sleeve, single- or double-row ball, or roller bearing type. In addition, some pumps use special thrust bearings to counteract high end thrust. Thrust bearings are normally used on multistage pumps that have high pressures and deliveries. On small horsepower pumps, the impeller and shaft frequently overhang the motor bearing. In such cases, all radial and axial thrust must be taken up by the motor bearings.

3.49　On large pumps, the motors are usually coupled to the pump shaft. The shaft is independently supported by one or two bearings, depending upon the design. Oil-lubricated bearings are usually provided with a separate oil sump. Some pump manufacturers use bearings that require grease. Bearings will be discussed in more detail in Chapter Ten.

3.50　*Shaft sleeves* are located on a pump shaft at the point at which the shaft passes through the stuffing box. The sleeve protects the shaft from wear by the packing or seals.

3.51　Shaft sleeves are usually made of high-carbon steel, stainless steel, or brass. Stainless steel is the most expensive, but will outlast the other types. Brass has the shortest life, but is easier to replace than the others. High-carbon steel is the hardest of the three to remove, and has a life span between the other two.

3.52   A shaft sleeve must be secured to the shaft on which it is installed in order to keep it turning with the shaft. Also, the sleeve must fit tightly enough to prevent leakage between the shaft and sleeve. Some sleeves are threaded onto the shaft. Others are keyed to the shaft with the key used to keep the impeller from rotating independently.

Chapter Four

Propeller and Turbine Pumps

Turbine Pump Introduction

4.01   The previous chapter presented quite a bit of information about end-suction and split-case centrifugal pumps and their applications. Although more end-suction centrifugal pumps are used in industry than any other type, they do have certain limitations. In some situations, such as in deep wells, their size limits their use. They also have limited capacity and efficiency. For certain applications, one of the various styles of turbine pump might be chosen.

4.02   Vertical turbine pumps are classified both by physical configuration and by flow pattern. The common physical configurations are:

- lineshaft turbines

- can turbines

- submersible turbines

- propeller pumps.

An example of each is shown in Fig. 4-1, on the following page, for comparison purposes.

Lineshaft Turbines

4.03   *Lineshaft turbines* are composed of four major parts, as shown in Fig. 4-2, on the following page.

Fig. 4-1. Common vertical turbine pumps

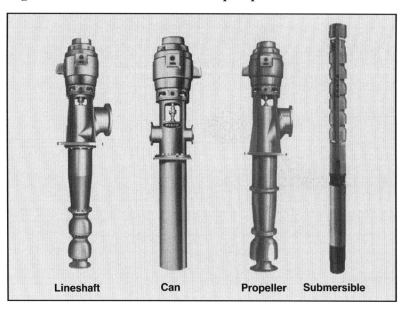

Lineshaft   Can   Propeller   Submersible

- the pumping unit

- the water column

- the discharge head

- the motor or drive unit.

Fig. 4-2. Lineshaft turbine

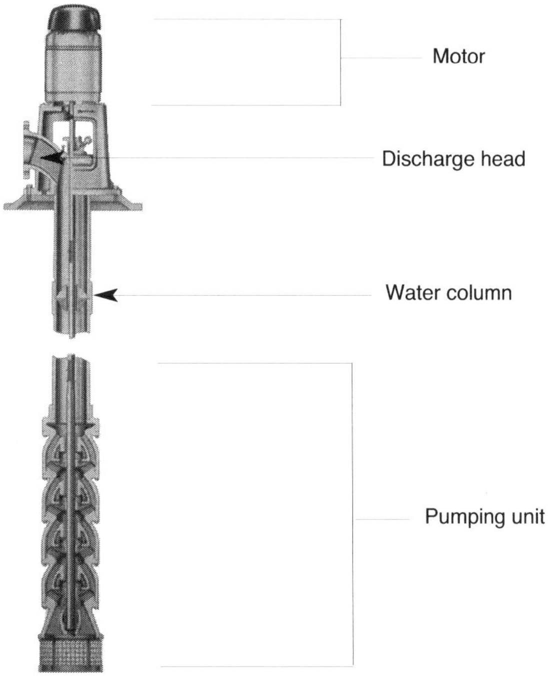

Motor

Discharge head

Water column

Pumping unit

4.04 The *pumping unit* (Fig. 4-3) consists of a *bowl assembly* and a *suction bell*. Fluid enters the pumping unit at the suction bell. It then passes to the bowl assembly, which consists of an impeller and a bowl or casing. The bowl surrounds the impeller and serves the same function as the volute of an end-suction centrifugal pump.

4.05 If the pump contains more than one bowl, as in Fig. 4-2, the pumped fluid passes upward through each bowl assembly. The amount of energy and pressure added to the fluid is directly proportional to the number of bowls. For example, if one bowl produces 50 psi, then two bowls will produce 100 psi, and three will produce 150 psi.

4.06 The amount of fluid pumped is not changed by the addition of pump bowls. The amount of fluid a pump can handle depends upon the capabilities of the first impeller.

4.07   The ability to add bowls to obtain high pressures makes this kind of pump very popular for use in deep wells in industry, irrigation, and municipalities.

4.08   The entire bowl assembly of a lineshaft turbine is usually submerged. Fluid travels from the bowl assembly through the *water column*. The column contains the drive shaft and radial bearings. These bearings help to keep the shaft aligned. They can be made of bronze or rubber.

4.09   Rubber bearings are usually water lubricated. Bronze bearings are usually oil lubricated. The oil-lubricated bearing generally works better in deep wells (over 300 ft). Some state regulatory agencies insist that oil-lubricated pumps not be used in municipal wells.

4.10   The column is secured to the *discharge head*. The pump discharge piping is connected to the discharge head. The discharge head contains the stuffing box. In water-lubricated pumps, the stuffing box contains either packing or a mechanical seal. Either can be used to control leakage around the shaft.

4.11   Because of the high pressures at which lineshaft turbines often operate, it is a common practice to use metal-core or metal-fiber packing. Such packing allows ample tightening of the packing without squeezing the lubricant from the packing. Shafts packed in this way last much longer than those packed with conventional packing.

4.12   When the pump uses oil-lubricated bearings, the drive shaft is fitted inside of a protective sheath that contains the bearings. With this arrangement, there is no packing material and no mechanical seal in the stuffing box. There should be no leakage from this type of stuffing box.

4.13   The *motor* is located above the discharge head. The common practice is to use hollow shaft motors on lineshaft turbines. The pump drive shaft passes through the motor shaft and is secured to the top of the motor by the head nut. This arrangement places the entire load of the drive shaft and impellers on the top bearing of the motor.

Fig. 4-3. Lineshaft turbine pumping unit

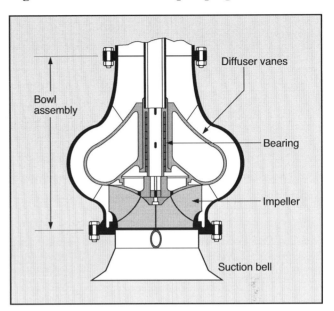

4.14   The motor's top bearing is referred to as the *thrust bearing* and is often a spherical-roller thrust bearing. The bottom bearing in this type of motor is commonly called the *radial bearing*. It is usually a single-row, deep-groove ball bearing.

4.15   The impellers used most often in lineshaft turbine pumps are either closed or semi-open. The semi-open impeller can be raised or lowered after pump installation to alter the pump capacity and discharge pressure. This adjustment is made by adjusting the head nut. It is for this purpose that the hollow-shaft motor was designed.

4.16   Adjustment of the impeller setting on semi-open impeller pumps can be critical. On one particular pump, for example, a change of 0.001 in. on the head nut can alter the discharge head 10 ft.

Can Turbines

4.17   The *can turbine* is an adaptation of the lineshaft turbine. It is often used as a booster pump, especially in municipal water systems. A can turbine pump is shown in Fig. 4-4. In this design, a lineshaft turbine is placed inside a metal or concrete "can." Fluid enters the can under pressure. The pump simply moves the fluid out of the can at a higher pressure.

4.18   This configuration can be confusing at first glance, because the inlet and outlet lines are commonly directly opposite one another. The incoming fluid is fed down into the can. The turbine inside the can pumps the fluid up and out the discharge port.

Submersible Turbines

4.19   Another version of the vertical turbine pump is the *submersible turbine*. This kind of pump is used in many individual homes and in municipal and industrial wells. A submersible turbine pump is shown in Fig. 4-5. The pump portion of this unit is similar to that of the lineshaft turbine. The major difference is that the motor is located under the pump instead of above it. The entire assembly is lowered into the fluid to be pumped. The fluid is used to cool the motor.

Fig. 4-4. Can turbine pump

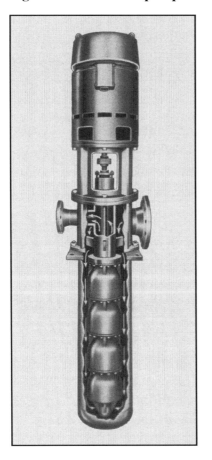

4.20 This pump's configuration eliminates the problems commonly associated with long drive lines and their bearings. It does cause other problems, however. If fluid enters the motor, the motor will fail. Also, you lose the ability to adjust the impeller clearance as you can with a lineshaft turbine.

Flow Patterns

4.21 As was mentioned earlier in this chapter, vertical turbines can be classified both by physical description and by flow pattern.

4.22 The lineshaft turbine, can turbine, and submersible pump are all classified as mixed-flow pumps. *Mixed flow* indicates several things.

- The fluid inside the pump does not flow straight up the shaft, as in an axial-flow pump.

- The fluid inside the pump does not make a right-angle turn as it flows through the impeller.

- Energy is transferred to the fluid being pumped in two ways—by centrifugal force and by a wedging action.

4.23 Another major style of vertical turbine is called a *propeller pump*. Propeller pumps can be classed as axial-flow or mixed-flow pumps. Mixed-flow propeller pumps move fluid partly by centrifugal force and partly by the lift of the blades or vanes on the fluid. Axial-flow propeller pumps move fluid only by the propelling or lifting action of the blades on the fluid.

4.24 The two separate designs, although they resemble each other outwardly, have different operating characteristics. Both axial-flow and mixed-flow propeller pumps are commonly installed with the entire pumping unit submerged.

Fig. 4-5. Submersible turbine pump

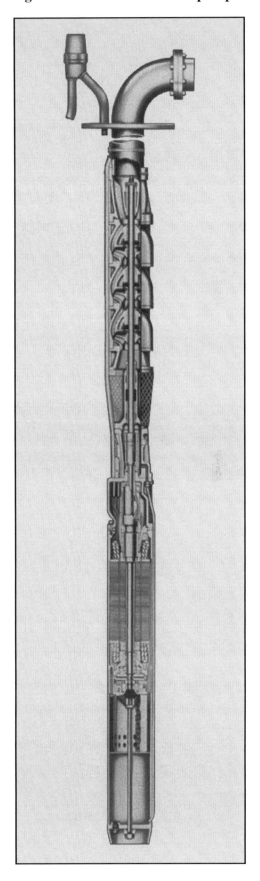

Fig. 4-6. Propeller pump

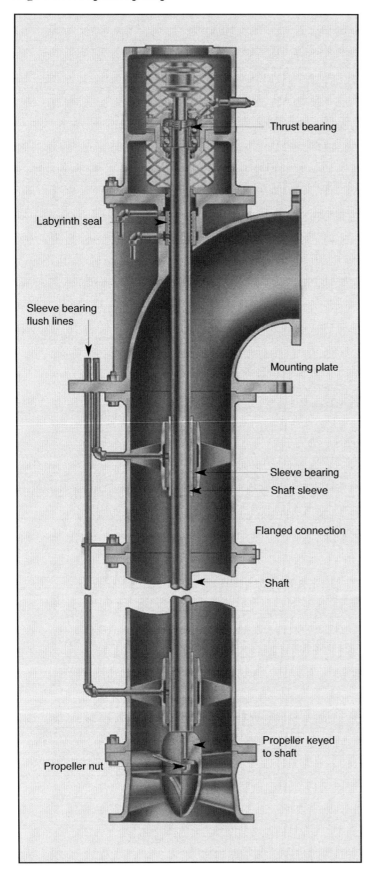

Thrust bearing

Labyrinth seal

Sleeve bearing flush lines

Mounting plate

Sleeve bearing
Shaft sleeve

Flanged connection

Shaft

Propeller keyed to shaft

Propeller nut

Axial-Flow Propeller Pumps

4.25   *Axial-flow propeller pumps* are often used to supply water for municipalities and irrigation purposes. They are also used for pumping out ponds or areas having excess amounts of water. These pumps normally deliver a high volume at low head, and are supported from the drive area. A typical axial-flow propeller pump is shown in Fig. 4-6.

4.26   The propeller pump bowl, as shown in cross section in Fig. 4-7, frequently resembles a short length of pipe. Generally, it is slightly smaller in diameter than the discharge pipe to which it is bolted. Often the pump bowl contains a set of *diffuser vanes*. The diffuser vanes reduce the stirring action caused by the pump propeller and thus straighten the flow of fluid into the discharge pipe.

4.27   In addition, the pump bowl contains one or two *steady bearings*. These bearings keep the shaft and impeller turning in a true line.

4.28   The suction bell is usually flared at the bottom. The bell might have diffuser vanes. Occasionally, an additional shaft steady bearing is built into the suction bell. The type and construction of the bell are determined by the application and by the manufacturer of the pump.

Mixed-Flow Propeller Pumps

4.29   A variation of the axial-flow propeller pump is the *mixed-flow propeller pump*. Although these two pumps are similar in design and in the type of materials used in construction, the impellers are quite different. An example of each type of impeller is shown in Fig. 4-8.

4.30   Unlike *axial-flow* impellers, which move the fluid parallel to the shaft, mixed-flow impellers give a slight swirling motion to the fluid as it leaves the impeller blades. The combination of axial and radial motion led to the *mixed-flow* classification.

4.31   Because of their design and the centrifugal action they impart, mixed-flow impellers are capable of attaining a slight suction lift. They are restricted, however, to impeller speeds above 4200 rpm. When operating at speeds below 4200 rpm, their operating efficiency decreases considerably.

4.32   The vanes of a mixed-flow impeller, which are enclosed in shrouds, discharge the fluid outwardly, much like an end-suction centrifugal pump. Although this kind of mixed-flow pump resembles a vertically mounted end-suction centrifugal pump, it is designed to handle much larger volumes of fluid.

4.33   Frequently the bowl assembly of a mixed-flow or axial-flow pump is cast slightly smaller than the discharge pipe. This construction permits the bowl and impeller to be removed up through the discharge pipe without dismantling the piping and supports. This feature is especially convenient when the pumps are down 20 ft or more and removing the piping and casing would require a great deal of time and special machinery. The smaller casing is connected to the larger discharge pipe by a split adapter ring. When the ring is removed, the casing can easily be pulled up through the discharge pipe.

Special Propeller Pumps

4.34   Although most axial- and mixed-flow propeller pumps operate with the impeller submerged in fluid, some propeller pumps are mounted horizontally and are located above the fluid's surface. Even when mounted in the horizontal position, the pump still has an end or bottom suction. Horizontally mounted pumps are limited in application and are only mentioned at this point to make you aware of their availability. Such a pump is shown in Fig. 4-9, on the following page.

Fig. 4-7. Axial-flow propeller pump bowl

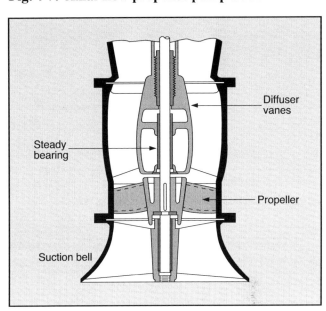

Diffuser vanes

Steady bearing

Propeller

Suction bell

Fig. 4-8. Propeller pump impellers

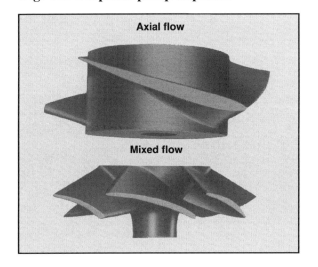

Axial flow

Mixed flow

Fig. 4-9. Horizontally mounted propeller pump

4.35　In applications involving high discharge heads, propeller pumps can be used in double or triple stages. Each stage will have the same propeller design. In operation, diffuser vanes direct the fluid discharged from one impeller into the suction of the next stage. This action boosts the fluid's pressure and velocity until it overcomes the head.

4.36　Although small, fractional horsepower sump pumps are usually of the end-suction centrifugal type, the larger sump pumps for sewage and slurry applications are often propeller pumps. Propeller pumps can handle much larger volumes of fluid than can end-suction pumps and generally are driven by motors of 5 to 10 hp or more.

Turbine Pump Construction

4.37　Vertical turbine pump suction bells and bowl assemblies can be made from a variety of materials. Usually, they are made of cast iron or steel. Pumps handling brine or chemically polluted water are usually made of stainless steel, bronze, or other noncorrosive alloys. Abrasion-resistant alloys are frequently used when the pumped fluid contains gritty material.

4.38　Pump impellers are usually made of cast materials similar to those used for the bowls. The choice of material depends upon the pump application and the compatibility of the impeller with the bowl material.

4.39　Because the impeller, bowl, and suction bell are usually located under water at all times, the selection of materials is important. If the wrong materials are selected, pump parts will corrode quickly, and unnecessary repairs will be required to keep the system in operation and pumping at peak efficiency.

4.40   In addition, if incompatible materials are used, a phenomenon called *electrochemical corrosion* can occur. Electrochemical corrosion causes pitting and material buildup on the pump's internal parts. It is most often a problem when the pumped fluid is high in dissolved solids. To counteract corroding and electrochemical action, special paints or surface coatings can be used.

4.41   The discharge head of a vertical turbine pump is usually made of fabricated or cast steel. Occasionally, more expensive alloy steels are used. Fabricated bronze or brass pipes are also used. The material selection depends upon the application.

4.42   The drive shaft, as shown in Fig. 4-10, extends down through the discharge pipe from the drive motor coupling. The drive shaft can be coupled directly to the drive motor by a splined hollow shaft, or with a flexible coupling. Depending upon the length, the shaft can be made of a single piece of steel or it can be made in sections.

4.43   Support bearings are sometimes located along the shaft to maintain alignment and to keep the shaft from deflecting as it rotates. The supporting bearings are often fastened to sides of the discharge pipe by diffuser vanes. These bearings can be made of rubber or bronze.

4.44   The shaft is normally sealed at the point at which it passes through the bend in the discharge pipe. The shaft might be sealed with packing or with a mechanical seal. In addition to the shaft seal, there are probably several guide vanes in the bend area to direct the flow of fluid around the bend smoothly. These guide vanes also direct the fluid pressure away from the shaft seal.

4.45   In some applications, the drive shaft is supported or contained within a separate housing in the discharge pipe. In such cases, the shaft and bearings operate in a dry atmosphere, except for the lubricant provided at the bearings.

Fig. 4-10. Turbine pump drive shaft and bearings

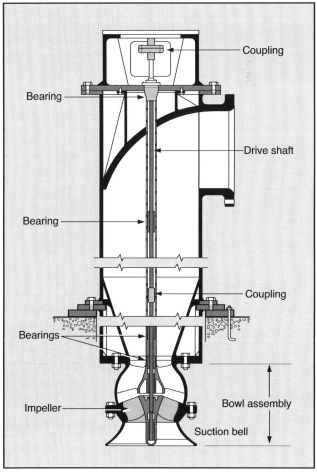

Vertical Turbine Pump Applications

4.46   Vertical turbine pumps vary in output capacity from 10 to over 25,000 gpm. In addition to pumping large quantities, these pumps are designed to operate under heads up to approximately 1000 ft.

4.47   The size and capacity of a vertical turbine pump are usually restricted by the diameter of the well in which it is placed. When used in wells, the pumps are also limited in capacity by the amount of fluid they can withdraw without depleting the supply in the pipe. The pumps are usually made up of two or more segments or stages, depending upon the well and the head requirements.

4.48   In addition to direct mounting in wells, vertical turbines are frequently mounted in a wet sump with a steady inflow of water. In these applications, the can turbine discussed earlier is used. The pump is often used to handle steam condensate and fresh water, and in so doing, frequently must pump against a high discharge head.

Regenerative Turbine Pumps

4.49   *Regenerative turbine pumps*, also called *periphery pumps*, are a unique version of centrifugal pump in which the impeller is a wheel with a large number of small vanes on both sides of the rim. A close-coupled, regenerative turbine pump is shown in Fig. 4-11. Figure 4-12 shows the pump's impeller and inner casing. The impeller rotates at a

Fig. 4-11. Regenerative turbine pump

Fig. 4-12. Regenerative turbine impeller

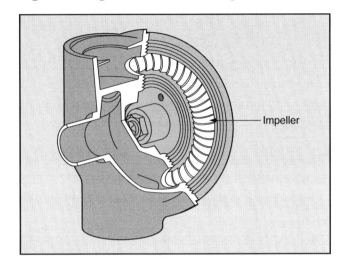

Fig. 4-13. Flow in a regenerative turbine pump

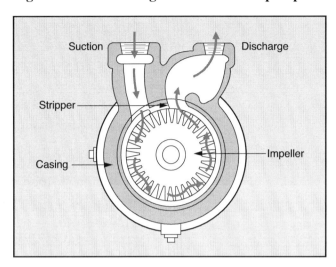

high speed (3600 rpm and up) in a ring-shaped channel in the pump's casing.

4.50   Some people refer to this kind of pump simply as a turbine pump. The term regenerative, however, describes more fully the action of the pump during its operation, and the method it uses to build up the required head. Component parts of these pumps are constructed of materials similar to those used in the pumps discussed previously.

4.51   Regenerative turbines are usually easy to recognize. Unlike the eccentric volute of an end-suction centrifugal pump, the case of a regenerative turbine is perfectly round. The suction and discharge are usually close together and of the same size pipe. These pumps can be either frame mounted or close coupled.

4.52   A relief valve is usually provided on the discharge side of the pump because of the high head pressures that can develop within the pump. The relief valve usually directs the discharged fluid back to the suction side of the pump.

4.53   As fluid enters the pump, a separator sends half of the fluid to each side of the impeller. The clearance between the edge of the impeller and the outside of the case is the same all around the case. The rotating impeller throws fluid toward the case, which directs it back to the impeller. This process is repeated as the fluid travels around inside the case, as shown in Fig. 4-13. When the fluid reaches the discharge port, it is forced out by a *stripper* between the suction and discharge ports.

4.54   Because of the close clearances between the impeller and the casing, regenerative turbines cannot be used to pump fluids containing grit or other solid particles. They can, however, pump fluids containing vapors or gases, providing there is enough liquid present to seal the close clearances.

4.55   Regenerative turbines can be used only to pump fluids with relatively low viscosities. Their life span is usually only a quarter that of a conventional centrifugal pump under similar operating conditions. Foreign materials in the pumped fluid or corrosion cause a rapid loss of capacity.

4.56   Regenerative turbine pumps are considered self priming, but are restricted in their capacities. Usually, they are manufactured as small pumps of less than 100 gpm with heads up to 500 ft. In applications requiring high-head capacities, the fluid delivery in gpm is relatively low. The horsepower required to drive the pump is higher at the high head pressures with low gpm. The horsepower drops, however, when the head pressure drops and the fluid delivery increases.

Chapter Five

Rotary Pumps

5

Introduction to Rotary Pumps

5.01   Rotary pumps are widely used for pumping high-viscosity fluids in marine fuel-oil service, fluid power applications, and crude oil and chemical processing. Although they are often thought of as viscous-fluid pumps, rotary pumps can handle fluids of all viscosities. They can deliver from less than 1 gpm to more than 5000 gpm at pressures of up to 10,000 psi.

5.02   Rotary pumps are positive-displacement machines that move fluid from pump inlet to pump outlet by trapping a portion of fluid between one or more moving elements and a fixed casing. The moving elements can be gears, cams, screws, vanes, or similar devices. Because rotary pumps deliver a given quantity of fluid with each revolution of the pump shaft, they can be adapted for metering applications.

5.03   Unlike centrifugal pumps, rotary pumps are usually self-priming and their delivery is not affected by pressure variations. They operate at much higher speeds than do reciprocating pumps, and are suitable for pumping nearly all nonabrasive fluids. They are usually simple, compact, and lightweight. Unlike reciprocating pumps, rotary pumps are capable of producing a flow that is free of pulsations.

5.04   The methods used to calculate rotary pump lift and head are similar to those used for centrifugal pumps. The fluid discharge is given in pounds per square inch rather than in feet of head, however, and the suction lift is given in inches of mercury. Impellers, casings, and shafts perform the same functions in both pumps, although their appearances may differ. The remainder of this lesson will examine several types of rotary pumps—their construction, operation, and application.

Fig. 5-1. Operation of an external-gear pump

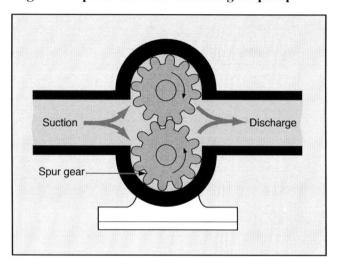

External-Gear Pumps

5.05   *External-gear pumps* are probably the most widely used type of rotary pump in industry today. Fluid power systems are frequent users of external-gear pumps. Many machine tools use external-gear pumps to supply bearing lubrication and cutting fluid to various points on the machine. The oil pumps in the engines of many vehicles are external-gear pumps. In addition, many pumps used in the chemical industry are external-gear pumps.

5.06   The operation of an external-gear pump is shown in Fig. 5-1. At first glance, you might think that the fluid being pumped is forced between the teeth of the two gears and pushed out the discharge port. As shown by the arrows in the illustration, however, the fluid is drawn into the space between the gear teeth and forced out of the discharge port. The meshing of the gears keeps fluid from flowing back to the pump's suction side.

5.07   Although spur-gear impellers are the most common kind used in gear pumps, helical and herringbone gears are sometimes used. Figure 5-2 shows pumps containing spur and helical gears. The pump shown in Fig. 5-3 contains herringbone gears. The kind of impeller used in a pump is determined by the pump manufacturer.

5.08   Helical and herringbone gears provide a smoother transfer of power than do spur gears, thus establishing a smoother fluid flow. For

Fig. 5-2. External-gear pump impellers

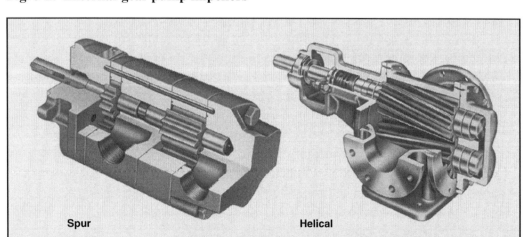

Fig. 5-3. Exploded view of an external-gear pump

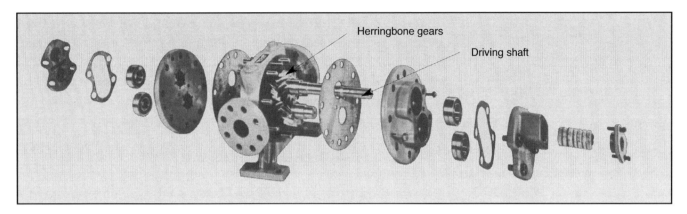

most applications, however, spur-gear impellers are satisfactory. They cost less to manufacture and maintain than other types. Helical and herringbone gears are used in pumps that handle larger capacities and operate at higher speeds than do spur-gear pumps.

5.09   In most applications, the slight discharge pulsations produced by spur gears do not warrant the use of specially designed gear impellers. Often the pulsations are damped by the fluid, which is being discharged under pressure.

5.10   The construction of an external-gear pump is relatively simple when compared to that of a centrifugal or turbine pump. Basically, the gear pump casing forms the external housing of the pump. It is usually made of cast iron or cast steel, although other metals can be used. Chemical pumps are often made of stainless steel.

5.11   Because external-gear pumps normally handle hydraulic or oily fluids, the bearings are lubricated not by external means but by the material being pumped. If the material being pumped is nonlubricating, seals and a method of external lubrication are used in the pump.

5.12   An exploded view of an external-gear pump is shown in Fig. 5-3. Notice that only one shaft extends beyond the end of the pump casing. This extended shaft is the driving shaft. The other is the shaft of the driven gear.

5.13   It is important to note that external-gear pumps, like most rotary pumps, are reversible. Most can operate in either direction without any modification in the internal parts of the pump or to the casing. If you are not sure which is the suction side of an operating pump, look to see which way the drive shaft is rotating. If you remember that the fluid being pumped is being carried around the outer edges of the gear impellers and not between them, you will be able to figure out which way the pump is pumping.

Fig. 5-4. Construction of an internal-gear pump

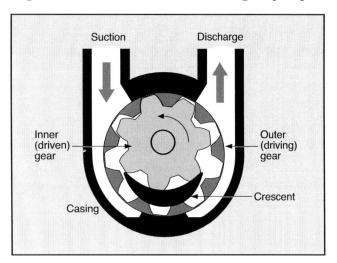

5.14 Because the pump casing encloses the operating parts of the pump, shaft seals are needed only at the extended drive shaft. Shaft seals can be of the mechanical or packing-gland type. The kind of shaft seal used is determined by the fluid being pumped, the design of the pump, and the application.

Internal-Gear Pumps

5.15 Another kind of gear pump is the *internal-gear pump*. This pump is entirely different in construction than the standard or external-gear pump.

5.16 The internal-gear pump, the construction of which is shown in Fig. 5-4, contains two meshing gears. The outer gear of the set is the driving gear. The inner gear is the driven gear. The *crescent* keeps the gears separated and reduces eddy currents, thus increasing the pump's efficiency. In some models the crescent is movable, allowing the pump to operate in either direction.

5.17 During operation, the rotating inner gear opens the space between the teeth of both gears at the intake port area. Fluid is drawn in through the intake port and passes around the crescent area of the pump, as shown in Fig. 5-5. As the gear teeth again come in contact with one another near the exit port, the fluid is discharged

Fig. 5-5. Fluid flow in an internal-gear pump

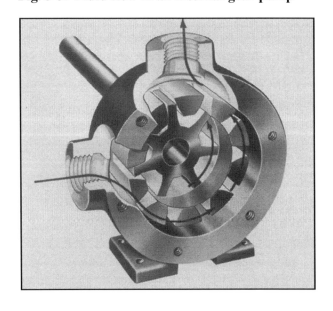

5.18 Even though the inner gear has fewer teeth than the outer gear, the gears mesh smoothly at all times without causing interference. This meshing occurs because the spacing of the gear teeth is equal, even though the pitch diameters are unequal.

5.19 The materials used in the construction of internal-gear pumps are similar to those used in external-gear pumps. The driving gear is usually made of steel. The driven gear can be made of steel or a softer metal. The pump casing is usually cast iron or steel, depending on the manufacturer's design. A single bearing supports the shaft where it comes through the casing. The shaft carries the driving gear. A bearing in the end cover supports the driven or internal gear.

Bearings for the two gears are positioned at the time the pump is manufactured. This allows for smooth meshing of the gears within the housing.

5.20 Because the driving gear contains and rotates around the driven gear, the housing is round and compact. This kind of housing is quite different from the elongated shape of the external-gear pump housing.

Lobe Pumps

5.21 *Lobe pumps* are similar to external-gear pumps in both construction and operation. The gears, however, are replaced by two rotors, each having one, two, three, or four lobes. One rotor is driven externally. Flow is less constant because a lobe pump delivers fluid in a smaller number of larger quantities than a gear pump. Figure 5-6 shows four types of lobe pumps.

5.22 The shape of lobed rotors does not allow one rotor to drive the other. For this reason, lobed rotors must be timed by separate means. *Timing gears* are used to transmit the torque from the driving rotor to the driven rotor. External timing of the lobe pump is necessary not only to drive the idler rotor, but also to maintain the proper angular relationship of the rotors.

Screw Pumps

5.23 *Screw pumps* can have one, two, or three screws or rotors operating within a close-fitting casing. The fluid being pumped flows between the screw threads or between the screw and the casing, along the

Fig. 5-6. Lobe pump construction

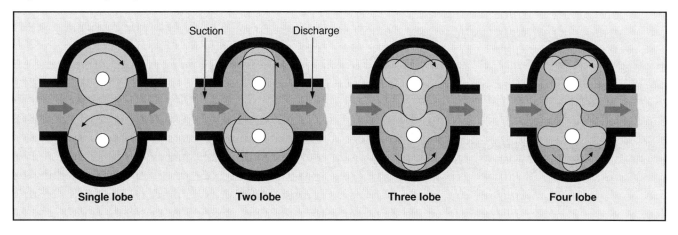

Fig. 5-7. Single-screw pump

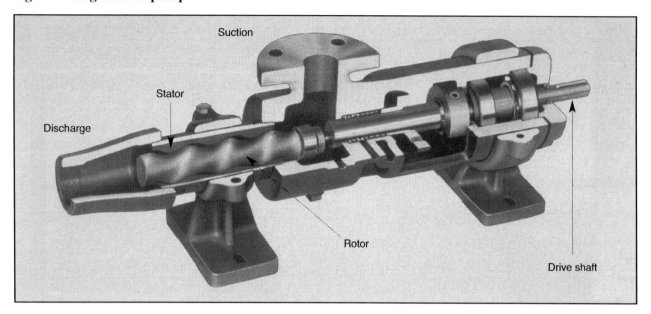

axis of the screws. Screw pumps can handle liquids of nearly any viscosity and can be operated at higher speeds than most other rotary pumps.

5.24 Most screw pumps do not handle abrasives well. Abrasive particles can cause jamming or accelerated wear between the rotors as the fluid moves along their mating surfaces. Abrasive materials can also damage the casing because of the small clearances between the casing and screws.

5.25 The simplest screw pump is the *single-screw pump*. It consists of a spiral-shaped rotor that turns in an internal-helix liner. The rotor is usually metal. The liner is rubber. Figure 5-7 shows a single-screw pump. The rotation of the screw traps fluid between the rotor and liner and moves it along the axis of the screw until it is discharged. Single-screw pumps are often called *progressing-cavity pumps*. Unlike other screw pumps, these pumps handle abrasives very well.

Fig. 5-8. Two-screw timed pump

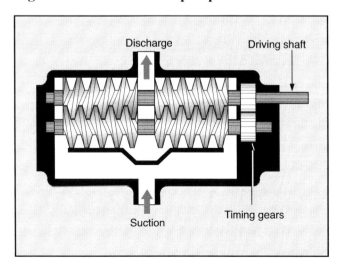

5.26 Multiple-screw pumps are driven by a single rotor called the *power rotor. Two-screw pumps* are often called *timed-screw pumps* because they require timing gears. If the pump will be used for pumping clean, lubricating fluids, the timing gears and bearings are often located within the pump casing, as shown in Fig. 5-8. In this arrangement, the fluid being pumped lubricates the gears and bearings. Because many fluids are nonlubricating or abrasive, external timing gears and lubrication are used most often. In screw pumps, timing gears transmit power from the driving shaft to the driven shaft without the necessity of screw contact. By eliminating the need for screw contact, timing gears promote long screw life.

5.27   *Three-screw pumps* have two idler screws. The idlers are threaded to mesh with the power rotor. Three-screw pumps are often referred to as *untimed- screw pumps,* because the driving force is transmitted by the rotors themselves, not by timing gears. In a three-screw pump, the center screw is the driving rotor. Often, the close-fitting housing provides the only support for the idler rotors.

5.28   Figure 5-9 shows a cutaway view of a three-screw pump. As the power rotor turns, fluid is drawn into the pump. Because the threads of the power rotor mesh with the threads of the idler screws, the fluid is forced along the openings in the threaded area toward the center discharge section of the pump.

5.29   A multiple-screw pump is manufactured with a solid center casing made from cast iron or steel. The interior of the casing is machined precisely to contain the rotors. The power rotor extends beyond one of the casing ends. The idler rotor shafts usually do not. Some type of seal is provided where the extended shaft passes through the pump end.

5.30   Rotors within a particular pump are usually made of the same material. High-carbon steel, steel alloy, and stainless steel are commonly used. The bearings supporting the shaft are usually sleeve bearings, and are either pressed onto the shaft or inserted and locked in place in the end or center casing.

Fig. 5-9. Three-screw pump

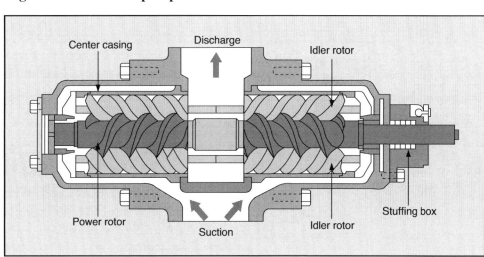

Vane Pumps

5.31   The *vane pump* is another type of rotary pump commonly used in industrial plants. Although generally used in hydraulic and lubricating oil systems, vane pumps are also used for solvent and chemical transfer. Vane pumps are often used for paint and other viscous materials and for other heavy fluids containing abrasive particles. For abrasive applications, the vanes are made of a softer material than the pump casing.

5.32   The vane pump shown in Fig. 5-10, called a *sliding-vane pump,* is simple in operation. As the impeller rotates, its offset position above the pump centerline allows the vanes to slide outward and draw fluid in on the inlet side. The open spaces between the vanes, impeller, and housing at the bottom of the pump allow movement of the fluid through the pump. As the impeller continues its rotation, the vanes are pushed back into their slots as they near the top of the pump. This constriction of available space forces the fluid out the discharge port.

5.33   The pump inlet and discharge ports are oval in shape and extend about three quarters of the way across the casing width. This less-than-full opening keeps the vanes within the pump casing. The oval shape smooths the fluid transfer.

5.34   Some vane pumps, called *swinging-vane pumps,* have a series of hinged vanes that swing out from the impeller as it rotates. These vanes trap fluid and force it out the discharge side of the pump. Still other vane pumps use rolling members. The operation of a *rolling-vane pump* is similar to that of the sliding-vane pump. The rolling action of the vanes, however, distributes wear and reduces sliding friction. Figure 5-11 shows a rolling-vane pump.

5.35   Vane pump housings, like those of other rotary pumps, are usually made of cast iron or cast steel. As in the internal-gear pump, the ends are machined smooth and the interior is bored in a circular shape.

5.36   The impeller is circular about its own centerpoint and is smaller in diameter than the housing. The impeller contains slots, which hold the vanes. The vanes are often metal, but can be made of molded neoprene or other soft materials. The vane material selected depends upon the material being pumped.

Fig. 5-10. Sliding-vane pump

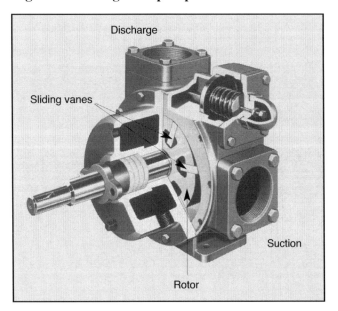

Fig. 5-11. Rolling-vane pump

Fig. 5-12. Location of seals on rotary pump shaft

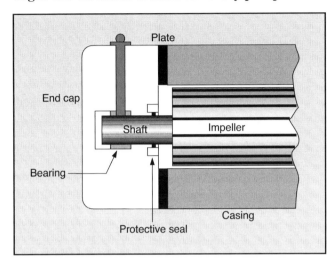

5.37   In sliding- and rolling-vane pumps, the vanes are mounted within the impeller with a small clearance to permit free movement. In some pumps, the impeller vanes are spring loaded at the base. The spring loading ensures complete contact with the pump housing at all times. In other pumps, the vanes are manually placed in position in the impeller. Centrifugal force and the hydraulic pressure within the pump keep the vanes in contact with the pump housing.

5.38   The end casings of the pump require careful positioning. Because the impeller shaft extends through one casing end and part way into the other, the shaft holes must line up accurately. Any misalignment between the two ends can cause the impeller to bind or jam within the casing.

5.39   Like the end casings in gear pumps, vane pump end casings are usually bushed with sleeve bearings. End casings can be fitted with lubrication fittings and seals if the application requires.

5.40   A vane pump handling paint is a good example of a pump requiring sealed bearings. The abrasive pigment in the paint would quickly destroy the pump bearings if it were allowed to come into contact with them. Seals at the interior edges of the end casing protect the bearings, as shown in Fig. 5-12. Lubrication is supplied through external fittings, because paint is not a lubricant. If the pump were handling a lubricant, a shaft seal would be required only at the point where the driving shaft extended through the end casing.

Rotary Piston Pumps

5.41   At the mention of piston pumps, many people immediately think of reciprocating piston pumps. There are also several kinds of rotary pumps called *piston pumps.* Although they all use some kind of piston element, they look and operate very differently from one another and from reciprocating piston pumps. Figure 5-13 shows three types of rotary piston pumps.

5.42   In the *circumferential-piston pump*, arc-shaped pistons travel on rotors in the pump housing. Its operation is similar to that of a lobe pump, except that the rotors do not mesh or even touch one another. Their only contact is with the walls of the pump casing.

5.43   Fluid is carried from the suction to the discharge port of the pump in the spaces between the pistons. Because the rotors do not contact one another, timing gears must be used.

5.44   In the *axial-piston pump,* piston elements reciprocate in cylinders in the pump rotor, parallel to the pump shaft. As the rotor rotates, the pumping action comes directly from the motion of the pistons. Unlike a reciprocating pump, this pump has no suction or discharge valves. Valving is accomplished by the rotation of the rotor relative to the suction and discharge ports. The angle of the cam plate determines the length of the piston stroke.

5.45   The *cam-and-piston pump* contains an eccentrically mounted cam rotated by a shaft in the center of a cylindrical casing. This cam moves a piston. Each rotation of the shaft traps fluid in the casing. As the rotation continues, the fluid is forced from the casing, through a slot in the piston, to the pump discharge.

Flexible-Member Pumps

5.46   In *flexible-member pumps*, the pumping and sealing action depend upon the flexibility of one of the pump's parts. This part might be the

Fig. 5-13. Rotary piston pumps

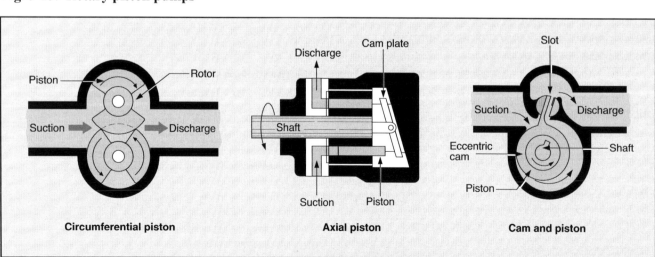

impeller, a tube, or a liner. The pumping element is usually made of rubber, synthetic rubber, or a plastic compound. Figure 5-14 shows three types of flexible-member pumps.

5.47   The pumping action of a *flexible-impeller pump* is similar to that of a vane pump. Instead of vanes sliding in and out of a rotor, however, blades bend against the pump casing.

5.48   Unlike the vane pump, which has a circular inner configuration, the inner shape of the flexible-impeller pump is irregular. This irregular shape increases the impeller's efficiency and gives the pump its ability to pump both thin and thick fluids.

5.49   As shown in Fig. 5-15, on the following page, the pump housing forms one of the end covers and contains the shaft support bearings, lubricant, and seals. The end cover has no impeller or shaft support bearings. Because of this construction, impeller replacement is relatively easy.

5.50   The *flexible-tube pump* operates on a principle similar to that of squeezing toothpaste from a tube by flattening or rolling the tube from the bottom. A flexible hose or tube passes through the pump body where it is flattened by a cam or rollers. Rotor rotation pushes the material in the tube from the suction to the discharge. The tube's recovery from its squeezed position creates a suction at the pump's inlet.

5.51   A flexible-tube pump can pump nearly any fluid as long as it is compatible with the tubing material. Since fluid contacts only the interior of the tube, it has no effect on the pump interior.

5.52   A *flexible-liner pump* is operated by an eccentric on a driven shaft. As the eccentric in Fig. 5-14 turns, it moves the flexible liner to the left, closing

Fig. 5-14. Flexible-member pumps

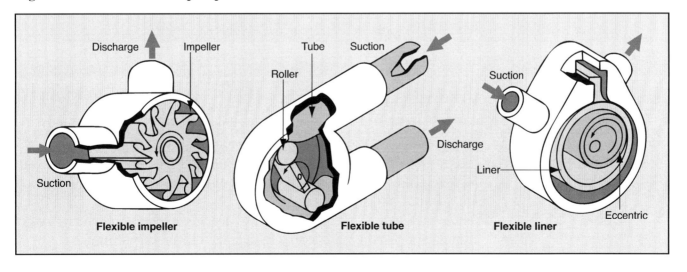

Fig. 5-15. Flexible-impeller pump

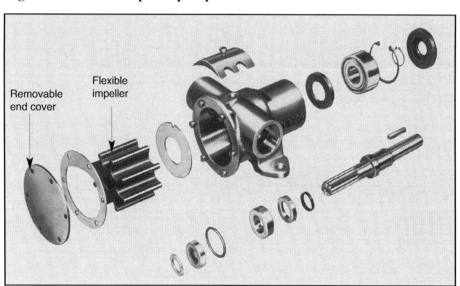

the suction and opening the discharge. As the eccentric continues, it squeezes the liner against the pump body, forcing the fluid out the discharge port. Flexible-tube and flexible-liner pumps are also called *peristaltic pumps.*

Rotary Pump Installations

5.53   Because rotary pumps are generally self-contained, having their own bearings and framework, they are usually installed as a separate piece of equipment and bolted to a bed plate or frame. They can be driven by any one of a number of prime movers, including electric motors, air motors, hydraulic motors, or internal combustion engines. Internal combustion engines are required for portable hydraulic pumping units that supply hydraulic fluids to several pieces of machinery mounted on the same structure. This arrangement is common in the construction machinery field. In-plant pumps are usually driven by electric motors. In hazardous atmospheres, the pump can be driven from a remote shaft or by special hazardous-duty motors.

5.54   When rotary pumps are motor driven, they are usually connected to the driving motor with a flexible coupling. In these applications, proper alignment between the shafts and couplings is extremely important if the pump is to operate properly. Misalignment causes excessive pump and motor bearing wear. This wear greatly reduces the operating life of the unit.

5.55   Gear and vane pumps are frequently used for manual pump applications. One familiar application is the hand-operated pump fitted with a suction pipe and placed directly in a 55-gallon drum. Other types of manual rotary pumps are used with lubricant-dispensing drums.

Chapter Six

Reciprocating Pumps

Reciprocating Pump Applications

6.01   At the mention of the term "reciprocating pump," maintenance people with many years of experience often think of steam-driven, piston-type water pumps. Although the use of these pumps has decreased over the years, many refineries and chemical plants still use steam-driven reciprocating pumps. Since such plants usually have steam available, these pumps are economical to operate. Because they are fireproof and explosionproof, steam-driven pumps are nearly ideal for pumping volatile or flammable liquids.

6.02   Many reciprocating pumps are driven by air pressure. These pumps, which are sometimes called *pneumatic pumps*, are often used to transfer fluids from barrels to other containers or to a piping system, which then carries the fluid to the machine requiring it.

6.03   Some reciprocating pumps are driven by a rotating crankshaft connected to an electric motor or internal combustion engine. These pumps are commonly called *power pumps*. Power pumps are well-suited to high-pressure service. They are often used in hydraulic presses, petroleum processing, boiler feeding, and pipeline pumping.

6.04   Other kinds of reciprocating pumps use a flexible diaphragm in the fluid end. *Diaphragm pumps* are commonly used in low-pressure metering applications, where freedom from leakage is important. Diaphragm pumps will be covered in detail in the following chapter.

6.05   Although all reciprocating pumps are similar in their pumping action, they vary greatly in construction. Figure 6-1, on the following page, shows an example of each of the three kinds of reciprocating pumps covered in this chapter.

Fig. 6-1. Typical reciprocating pumps

Reciprocating Pump Parts

6.06   A reciprocating pump works with a back-and-forth, straight-line motion. A reciprocating pump driven by an air- or steam-driven piston is called a *direct-acting pump*. Direct-acting pumps have two sections—the *fluid end* and the *steam* or *air end*. The fluid end does the pumping. The steam or air end provides the driving force necessary for operating the fluid end. Figure 6-2 shows a direct-acting, steam-driven piston pump.

6.07   In power pumps, the two sections are called the *fluid end* and the *power end*. The fluid end does the pumping. The power end provides the

Fig. 6-2. Direct-acting, steam-driven piston pump

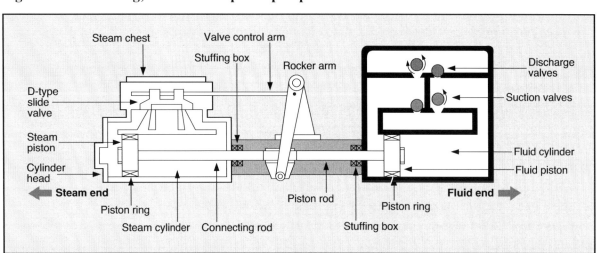

pumping force. The power end consists of a crankshaft, a crosshead, and a connecting rod. Figure 6-3 shows a typical power pump.

6.08   Many pump parts are called out in Fig. 6-2 and Fig. 6-3. The following paragraphs describe some of the most important ones. Refer to the illustrations as you come to each new term.

6.09   **Piston.** Fluid-end pistons convert mechanical energy into fluid movement. In the steam end of the direct-acting pump, the piston converts the steam into mechanical energy.

6.10   **Piston ring.** A piston ring acts as a seal between a piston and the cylinder in which it is operating. The ring moves with the piston.

6.11   **Plunger.** Some pumps, like the one shown in Fig. 6-3, use a plunger rather than a piston in the fluid end. The plunger slides back and forth in a stationary packing rather than carrying its own seal.

6.12   **Cylinder.** The cylinder is a tubular chamber that contains the piston or plunger.

6.13   **Cylinder head.** The cylinder head is a cap that seals the cylinder to allow pressure buildup.

6.14   **Stuffing box.** A stuffing box is filled with packing to prevent fluid leakage from the cylinder. It surrounds the plunger, piston rod, and connecting rod.

6.15   **Valves.** A slide valve controls the flow of steam into the steam end of the direct-acting pump. On the fluid end of the pump, suction and

Fig. 6-3. Power plunger pump

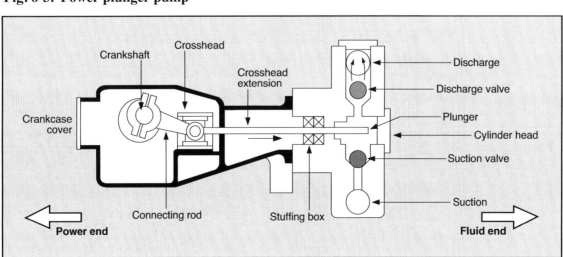

discharge valves control the flow of fluid into and out of the fluid cylinder. The valve on the steam end is mechanically actuated. The valves on the fluid end are material actuated.

6.16   **Crankshaft.** In the power pump, the crankshaft transmits motion from the prime mover to the driving components in the power end of the pump.

6.17   **Crosshead.** The crosshead of the power pump converts the rotary motion of the crankshaft connecting rod into reciprocating motion.

Reciprocating Pump Classifications

6.18   You have read so far that reciprocating pumps can be classified in different ways. They can be direct-acting or power pumps, piston or plunger pumps. They are also classified as horizontal or vertical.

6.19   Reciprocating pumps can be classified in other ways. One involves the pumping action in the fluid end. A *single-acting pump* (Fig. 6-3 is an example) discharges fluid only on the forward stroke of the plunger. The return stroke is a cylinder-loading stroke and does not discharge any fluid into the discharge line. Pumps of this type discharge fluids in pulses.

6.20   *Double-acting pumps*, like the one shown in Fig. 6-2, discharge fluid on both strokes of the piston. As the piston travels to one end of the pump, fluid is discharged from that end of the cylinder. While this is happening, fluid is drawn in on the other side of the piston. When the piston reverses its travel, the side of the pump that just loaded discharges its fluid, and the other side of the pump draws fluid in. Although double-acting pumps are more efficient than single-acting pumps, they still have a slight pulsation in the fluid flow as the piston reaches the end of its stroke.

6.21   Another means of classifying pumps involves the number of fluid-end cylinders. A *simplex pump* is a single-cylinder pump. It has only one fluid cylinder.

6.22   A *duplex pump* is a two-cylinder pump. It usually consists of two simplex pumps mounted side by side in a common housing. Duplex pumps are usually double acting. The resulting pump capacity is twice that of a simplex double-acting pump.

6.23   Duplex pumps generally have piston travels that oppose each other. This does not mean that the pistons work against each other. When the piston in one cylinder is traveling forward, the piston in the other cylinder is traveling in the opposite direction. This process is illustrated in Fig. 6-4.

Fig. 6-4. Piston action in a duplex pump

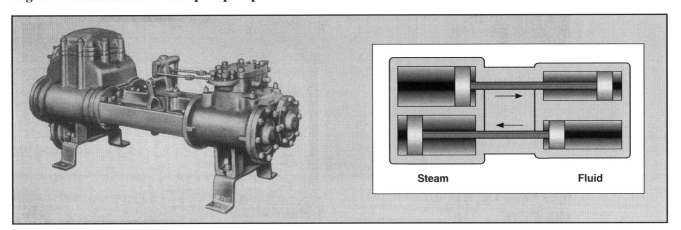

Steam   Fluid

6.24   Some pumps are made in triplex and multiplex designs. These pumps, which have three or more cylinders, are not often used in industrial plants. They are mentioned at this point so that you will know the meaning of the words. Figure 6-5 shows a complete classification chart of reciprocating pumps.

Steam-Driven Pump Operation

6.25   Figure 6-6, on the following page, shows a steam-driven reciprocating pump. Although steam-driven pumps might vary in appearance, their operating characteristics are usually similar. The only differences are in the valves and body construction.

6.26   Most steam-driven reciprocating pumps discharge fluids at pressures from approximately 125 to 750 psi. Fluid capacities range from 200 to over 1200 gpm. These pumps are suitable for hot or cold service with only slight modifications in their component parts.

Fig. 6-5. Classification of reciprocating pumps

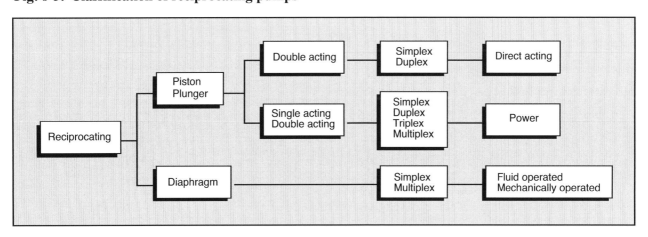

Fig. 6-6. Steam-driven reciprocating pump

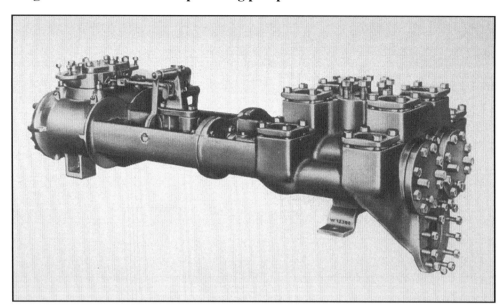

The Fluid End

6.27   Figure 6-7 shows two cross sections of the fluid end of a horizontal, steam-driven pump. Because the cylinder is double acting, there are two sets of valves and the cylinder is open at both ends. If this cylinder were single acting, it would probably be open on only one end, with the fluid inlet located on that side of the piston. In some pumps, the fluid is drawn in at the bottom of the cylinder and discharged out of the top of the cylinder. The construction used depends upon the manufacturer.

6.28   Notice how the valves are positioned in the fluid end of the pump. In operation, fluid is drawn in through one suction valve as the piston travels away from that end of the cylinder. When the piston reverses its travel, the fluid pressure within the cylinder closes the intake valve and forces the fluid

Fig. 6-7. Fluid end of a double-acting, steam-driven pump

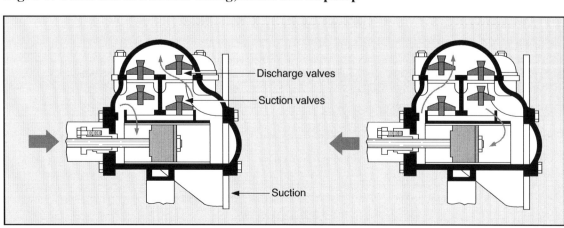

out of the discharge valve. When the piston again reverses its travel, the discharge valve is closed by a combination of discharge line pressure and spring action on the valve. The intake valve again opens to admit fluid.

6.29   The valves on the fluid end of the pump fall into two categories—*valve plate* and *pot valve*. The general construction and operation of the two types are similar. Their mounting, however, is different.

6.30   Pumps with fluid ends of the valve-plate design, as shown at the left in Fig. 6-8, are frequently referred to as *submerged-piston pumps*. This term is used when the discharge valves are positioned above the piston. In this arrangement, a quantity of fluid remains in the cylinder at the end of the discharge stroke.

6.31   In pumps of the pot-valve design, shown at the right in Fig. 6-8, the discharge valves are mounted to one side of the cylinder. The fluid being pumped is still not completely discharged from the cylinder, but less fluid remains than in the valve-plate pump.

6.32   In both the valve-plate and pot-valve designs, the intake valves are located above the cylinder to allow easy flow of fluid into the cylinder during the pump's intake stroke.

6.33   Most manufacturers of these pumps allow the valves to be used interchangeably. This flexibility reduces the stock of maintenance parts and simplifies maintenance procedures.

6.34   Fluid cylinders in reciprocating pumps often have renewable liners. Generally, the liners are made of cast iron or steel, but can be made of abrasion-resistant materials. The material used depends upon the fluid being pumped. Liners are pressed in place. Occasionally, they require additional holding lugs to keep them from moving.

Fig. 6-8. Fluid end valve designs

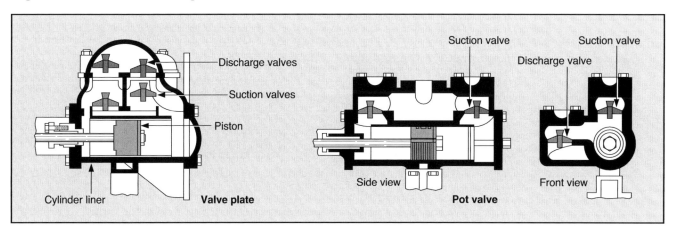

6.35   Fluid-end pistons are usually made of cast iron. They carry piston rings to keep fluid from leaking past the piston. The rings are usually made of soft iron or steel, but their composition varies as required for specific pumping applications.

The Steam End

6.36   The steam end of the cylinder is made of cast iron or steel and is not equipped with a liner. Liners are unnecessary in the steam end, because the amount of wear that takes place between the piston and the cylinder is slight. Most of the wear on the fluid end is caused by the contaminants within the fluids being pumped or by the abrasive nature of the material.

6.37   The piston rings on the driving end are made of cast iron. They are usually self-adjusting and are supplied in sets of two or more for each piston.

6.38   The slide valve controlling the steam flow is a simple mechanism. Basically, it is a flat plate with several slots or grooves in the face that contacts the pump body.

6.39   In operation, steam is continuously admitted to the center portion of the pump valve. The valve then directs it to one of the two sides of the piston, forcing the piston to move to one side or the other. As the piston travels, the valve control arm attached to the connecting rod moves the slide valve in the opposite direction. This action causes the slide valve to direct the steam to the opposite side of the piston when the piston reaches the end of its stroke.

Power Pump Operations

6.40   Power pumps are usually driven by electric motors. They can also be driven by internal combustion engines. The drive can be connected directly to the pump crankshaft, or the connection can be made through a speed reducer. These pumps range in size from relatively small units, rated at 20 gpm or less, to large units, with capacities of several thousand gallons per minute.

6.41   The pressure-range capability of these pumps is great. It varies from several hundred pounds per square inch to over 20,000 psi. Because of the high discharge-pressure capability of these pumps, you must be extremely cautious when servicing them. Make certain the pressure is relieved before disconnecting any of the lines. These high-pressure pumps are usually used for hydraulic cleaning and descaling operations in steel mills and chemical plants. They are also used to drive hydraulic presses in plastic molding and extruding processes.

Horizontal Plunger Pumps

6.42   Power pumps are made in two general designs. The horizontally mounted plunger pump uses a plunger to pump the fluid. Compared to a piston, the plunger is quite long and operates into a relatively open cavity. The end of the plunger might even extend into the cavity at the end of its discharge stroke. The photo at the right in Fig. 6-9 shows a horizontal plunger pump.

6.43   The intake and discharge valves are similar to those used in other reciprocating pumps and, like them, are fluid operated. The valves are sometimes spring loaded to allow for easier closing.

6.44   The driven end of the plunger is threaded or tapped so that it can be attached to the connecting rod. The connecting rod, which travels in a straight line, is connected to a crosshead. The crosshead stabilizes the movement of the plunger and converts the rotary motion of the crankshaft connecting rod to the reciprocating motion of the plunger.

6.45   The fluid being pumped lubricates the fluid end of the pump. The power end of the pump normally operates in an independent oil bath.

Fig. 6-9. Power plunger pumps

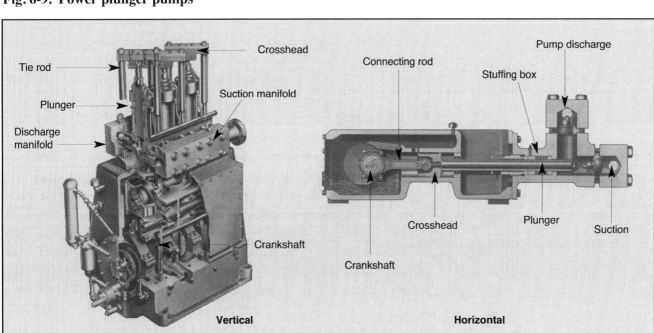

Vertical Plunger Pumps

6.46   The other style of power pump is larger than the horizontal pump and is mounted in a vertical position, as shown at the left in Fig. 6-9. The power end of this pump contains a crank-shaft and crosshead and is similar in operation to the horizontally mounted pump. The fluid end of the pump uses a plunger to pump the fluid, but it is unlike the horizontal pump in construction and operation.

6.47   The plunger is connected to a movable frame, which controls its movement. The frame is mounted on top of the pump body and is bolted to the crosshead. The tie rods connecting the frame and crosshead are stabilized as they pass through the upper portion of the pump frame. When operating, the plunger travels vertically in the cylinder, drawing in and discharging fluid.

6.48   Lubrication of vertical plunger pumps is similar to that of horizontal units. Additional lubrication should be provided at the points where the frame tie rods pass through the upper portion of the pump housing and at the crossheads. The pump is lubricated by the splash and pressurized methods.

Air-Driven Pump Operation

6.49   Air-driven reciprocating pumps are usually vertically mounted and are similar in design, construction, and operation. The pumps differ only in the control methods of the air and fluid. Two different types of air-driven pumps are shown in Fig. 6-10.

6.50   The efficiency of air-operated pumps depends upon free, continuous operation. When there is excessive back pressure at the discharge port or the fluid is stopped or slowed, the pump will stall until the discharge line is opened again. This stalling occurs in grease guns used for lubrication. When the trigger of the gun is pulled, the grease flows and the pump operates. When the gun trigger is released, the grease flow ceases and the pump stops.

6.51   The pistons that drive these units vary in size, which provides a useful ratio between the driving and pumping ends. For example, if the pistons on the fluid and air ends are of equal diameter, the ratio is one to one (1:1). If the area of the air piston is 10 in^2 and the area of the fluid piston is 1 in^2, the ratio is ten to one (10:1). The ratio does not affect fluid flow as long as the air pressure remains constant. If the air pressure drops below that which is required to pump the fluid, the pump will stall or operate at decreased flow. This ratio does increase the pressure of the fluid being discharged.

Fig. 6-10. Air-driven reciprocating pumps

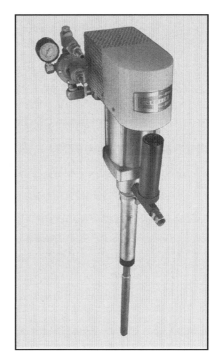

6.52   Fluid discharge pressure is simple to calculate. If the pump has a 10:1 ratio and the motor air supply is 80 psi, the discharge pressure of the fluid is 800 psi. If one air motor drives two pumps at the same time, the pressure on each pump is one-half the total.

The Fluid End

6.53   Because most air-driven pumps contain only a single cylinder, they are usually of the double-acting type. As shown in Fig. 6-11, the fluid end is constructed very differently from those of the pumps previously discussed. Note that the pump has two separate cylinders. The lower cylinder is larger in diameter than the upper cylinder. Each cylinder has its own piston. The discharge capacity of the pump is based on the area of the upper cylinder rather than on the area of the lower cylinder.

6.54   At the start of operation, the lower piston draws in fluid on the upstroke through the valve (ball or disk) located in the bottom of the pump. This motion fills the lower part of the cylinder. As

Fig. 6-11. Air-driven pump, fluid end

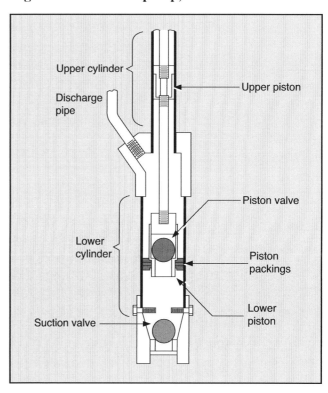

the pump stroke reverses and travels downward, the pressure of the fluid in the lower part of the pump closes the bottom valve and opens the valve in the piston. The fluid then flows into the upper chamber of the cylinder.

6.55   As the pump reverses its stroke and again travels upward, more fluid is drawn into the lower part of the cylinder through the bottom valve. The valve in the lower piston closes, and the upward travel of the piston forces some of the fluid in the upper part of the cylinder out into the discharge pipe. The rest of the fluid remains in the upper cylinder, below the upper piston.

6.56   When the piston reverses for the downstroke, the upper piston forces some of the fluid in the upper cylinder out of the discharge pipe. At the same time, the valve in the lower piston opens from the force of the fluid captured behind it, and admits more fluid to the upper part of the lower cylinder. Because of this construction, this type of pump discharges fluid on both the upstroke and the downstroke.

6.57   Fluid cylinders are usually made of aluminum, steel, or stainless steel tubing. In high-pressure pumps, the pump cylinders are manufactured from heavy-duty steel or stainless steel shafting bored to the proper inside diameter.

6.58   The pistons, connecting rods, and other internal components of the pump are normally made of stainless steel or corrosion-resistant steel alloys.

6.59   The piston packings are usually made of leather, neoprene, nylon, or Teflon®. The type of packing used is determined by the fluid being pumped. In most applications, leather packings give the best service. Note that the lower piston packings are positioned so that one is turned up and the other is turned down. They are set this way because fluid is being pumped on both strokes. In the upper cylinder, all packings are turned toward the fluid side of the pump.

The Air End

6.60   The air end of an air-driven pump is a simple piece of equipment. It consists of a brass or steel cylinder made from tubing that has sufficient strength to withstand the air pressure. The piston is a simple plate-type piston. It carries two piston rings or cups (usually leather) mounted facing away from each other to seal the piston.

6.61   The air control valve is probably the most complicated and critical part of the pump's air end. Although air control valves are made in several

®Teflon is a registered trademark of E.I. du Pont de Nemours & Co., Inc.

styles, they all operate on similar mechanical principles. Figure 6-12 shows the air end of a typical pneumatic pump.

6.62 A small control rod connects the air control valve to the piston. As the piston nears the end of the downstroke, the air control rod contacts and shifts the position of the air control valve on top of the pump. This shifting either opens or closes the air control valve ports, depending on their arrangement. Opening the port, in this case, admits air to the bottom side of the piston. At the same time, the upper air control port closes and vents the top side of the piston to the atmosphere.

6.63 As the piston travels upward and approaches the top of the stroke, the control rod again shifts the valve and closes off the air to the lower portion of the cylinder. At the same time it opens the air inlet valve to the upper portion of the cylinder. The lower air control port then releases the air to the atmosphere.

Fig. 6-12. Air-driven pump, air end

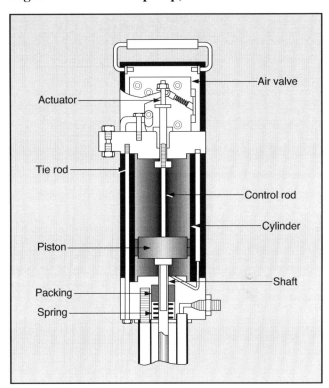

6.64 As mentioned earlier, this pump will stall if the flow of fluid in the discharge line is restricted. When the flow in the discharge line is restricted, the pressure on the fluid end quickly becomes equal to the pressure of the air coming in on the air end. Since the piston cannot reverse its direction until it reaches the end of its stroke, the pump stalls.

6.65 The cylinder ends are usually bolted to the cylinder by tie rods, although some are threaded. The cylinder is sealed by O-rings inserted between the cylinder wall and the cylinder ends.

6.66 Air-driven pumps usually have a stuffing box located between the air and fluid ends at the point at which they meet beneath the air cylinder. This stuffing box not only seals the air cylinder, but also prevents any fluid that gets past the fluid stuffing box from reaching the air cylinder. Most manufacturers also provide an overflow outlet near the top of the fluid end of the pump. This outlet allows any fluid that gets past the stuffing boxes to discharge back into the fluid end.

Chapter Seven

Metering Pumps

7

Introduction to Metering Pumps

7.01   Although metering pumps frequently resemble other kinds of pumps, they are very special in their design and construction. A *metering pump* displaces a specified volume of fluid in a specified period of time. These positive-displacement devices are also known as *controlled-volume, proportioning,* or *chemical reagent injection pumps.*

7.02   Because of the precision of their construction, metering pumps are very sensitive to temperature changes in the fluids they handle. In addition, they are easily affected by jarring, bumping, and vibration. You must take special care to protect the adjustable mechanisms that control the flow rate.

7.03   Most metering pumps are designed with a very close fit between the pump casing and the internal parts. To maintain this close fit, the fluid being pumped is usually filtered or strained before it enters the pump. If the pump is metering paints, slurries, or other materials containing solids, larger clearances are built into the pump.

Metering Pump Classifications

7.04   Most metering pumps are reciprocating pumps. They are classified in one of two ways, according to the design of their fluid ends—as either plunger (or piston) pumps or diaphragm pumps. An example of each of these two kinds of pumps is shown in Fig. 7-1, on the following page.

7.05   The fluid-end assemblies, valves, and stroke-adjustment mechanisms of reciprocating metering pumps are the elements that

Fig. 7-1. Reciprocating metering pumps

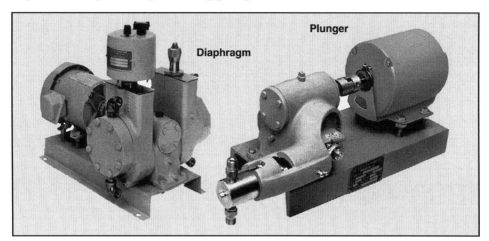

distinguish them from other reciprocating pumps. Such specialized elements give these pumps the capability of zero leakage and accurate flow adjustment.

7.06   Although reciprocating pumps are the type most often chosen for metering purposes, rotary pumps are sometimes used. Three types of rotary metering pumps are shown in Fig. 7-2.

7.07   Metering pumps are usually driven by an external power source, which can be at constant or variable speed. If a variable-speed drive is used, the flow rate of the pump changes with pump speed. In other pumps, flow rate is adjusted mechanically within the pump.

Fig. 7-2. Rotary metering pumps

7.08   Some reciprocating metering pumps are air-driven. The fluid ends of these pumps are similar to the fluid ends of other reciprocating metering pumps. The power ends, however, are different. Instead of being driven by a rotating crank, these pumps are driven by compressed air.

7.09   The terms used to describe the various parts of metering pumps are the same as those used with the general-purpose, positive-displacement pumps described in earlier chapters. Definitions are given in this chapter only when the parts are unique to metering pumps or different from those previously discussed.

Plunger and Piston Metering Pumps

7.10   The basic design and construction of a plunger metering pump are similar to those of a typical industrial plunger pump. Changes, if any, are usually in the driving end of the pump, although some modifications can be made to the fluid end for pumping specific fluids.

7.11   The pump housing is mounted independently of the drive mechanism. An externally mounted connecting rod connects the pump plunger to the gear reducer or motor. On this type of pump, the connecting rod is usually adjustable at the crankshaft. Adjustment of the connecting rod varies the amount of fluid pumped.

7.12   On some pump models, connecting rods are threaded at the point at which the rod is attached to the plunger. This additional fine adjustment gives the metering plunger the ability to regulate the fluid being pumped more precisely.

7.13   The adjustable connecting rod is usually *calibrated* (marked with graduations) to indicate the length of the plunger stroke. Marking can also indicate the amount of fluid that will be pumped with each stroke of the plunger.

7.14   When operating, a metering pump can discharge fluids in amounts ranging from 0 to over 20 gpm. The amount of fluid that can be pumped varies with the size and type of pump. Systems that require larger capacities often use more than one pump.

7.15   A detailed view of the fluid end of a plunger metering pump is shown in Fig. 7-3, on the following page. You can see the construction of the body, plunger, plunger packing, and the check valves. Because this is a reciprocating pump, a crosshead or plunger support is located at the rear of the fluid end. This crosshead stabilizes the motion of the plunger and eliminates unusual loading or wear between the plunger and the body.

Fig. 7-3. Plunger pump fluid end

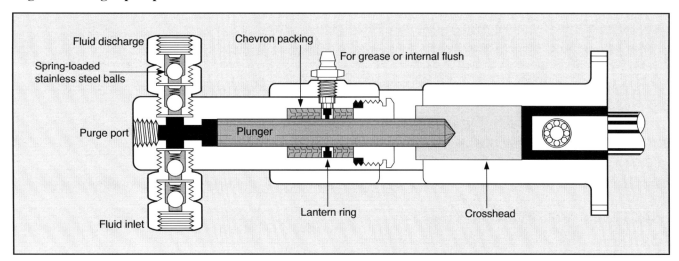

7.16   Most pump bodies and plungers are made of stainless steel or other corrosion-resistant alloys. Usually, the clearance between the plunger and the pump body is very small. In many cases, the plunger and the pump body are *lapped* (ground or polished as a set or pair) to ensure a close fit. This close fit eliminates leakage within the pump and helps to meter the fluid discharge accurately.

7.17   The plunger in this pump is packed with chevron packing. *Chevron packing* has a V-shaped cross section. The packing material might be rubber, neoprene, nylon, Teflon®, or some other material, depending upon the fluid being pumped. An adjustable packing gland is usually placed at the rear of the fluid end to maintain pressure on the packing, thereby preventing leakage. For more details on packing and seals, see Chapter Nine.

7.18   Figure 7-3 shows the plunger recessed within a cylinder that has a remote check valve area. Some pump designs allow the plunger to extend into the check valve area. The particular design depends upon the manufacturer and on the fluid being pumped.

7.19   Like other piston and plunger pumps, the intake and discharge valves of reciprocating metering pumps are moved by the material being pumped. The particular model shown in Fig. 7-3 uses two check valves on both the intake and discharge side of the pump. This double check valve system ensures fluid control at all times and minimizes the possibility of both check valves being held open by material jammed around the seat area. The check valves shown are ball valves. Some pumps use disk valves.

7.20   Most check valves are made of stainless steel, but they can be made of chrome-plated alloy steel. No matter what material is used, the

®Teflon is a registered trademark of the E. I. du Pont de Nemours & Co., Inc.

valves are polished to a smooth finish to ensure positive seating when the valve closes. In many piston and plunger pumps, the valves are closed by springs as well as the pressure of the fluid acting on them.

7.21   Most metering pumps are lubricated by the fluid they pump. Some pumps have additional lubrication points in the packing area. These points provide lubricant to areas of the pump that normally do not contact the pumped fluid. Use care in lubricating these parts to avoid overlubrication.

7.22   Some pumps cannot be lubricated by the fluid they are pumping. If a pump is switched from one installation to another, you must determine if the lubricant in the pump body and the seal or stuffing box is compatible with the new fluid before any new fluid is added to the pump. If the lubricant is not compatible, it must be removed and the seals or packing replaced.

7.23   Figure 7-4 shows a vertically mounted piston metering pump. This particular pump is the heart of a force-feed lubricator that pumps small amounts of oil to machinery injection points. The lubricator consists of a steel reservoir that contains the oil to be pumped. A camshaft inside the reservoir operates the single-piston pump. All working parts are enclosed, so they remain free from dirt, water, and other impurities. The pump parts are lubricated by the fluid in the reservoir.

Fig. 7-4. Vertically mounted piston metering pump

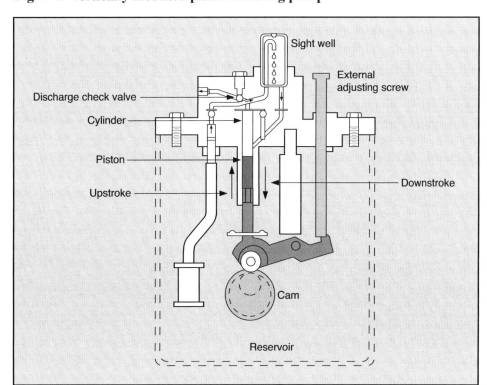

7.24   Rotation of the lubricator's cam operates the piston in the reservoir. On the piston's downstroke, lubricant is drawn into the cylinder from the sight well. This creates a vacuum in the airtight sight well, which causes lubricant from the reservoir to be drawn into the well until the pressure is equalized. On the piston upstroke, the oil in the cylinder is ejected through the discharge check valve to the machine injection point. The number of drops seen falling into the sight well is the amount of oil discharged by the pump. The pump can be adjusted by an external screw. This adjustment changes the length of the piston stroke, which changes the pump discharge volume.

Diaphragm Pumps

7.25   Most diaphragm metering pumps use hydraulic pressure delivered by a piston to actuate the diaphragm. Under these conditions, the pump diaphragm has fluid on both sides, as illustrated in Fig. 7-5. The side that produces the pumping action is called the *power side,* while the side doing the pumping is called the *fluid side.*

7.26   Because the diaphragm is flexible, it reacts to any pressure exerted on it by outside forces. Diaphragms are designed to withstand maximum flexing and to prevent penetration by the fluids being pumped. Some diaphragms have metal backup plates called *disk plates* to prevent excessive flexing.

7.27   As hydraulic fluid is forced against the power side, the diaphragm flexes away. This motion discharges the fluid on the fluid side of the diaphragm. This pressure closes the suction check valve. As the pump piston retracts, the hydraulic fluid is withdrawn from the power side. The

Fig. 7-5. Diaphragm pump operation

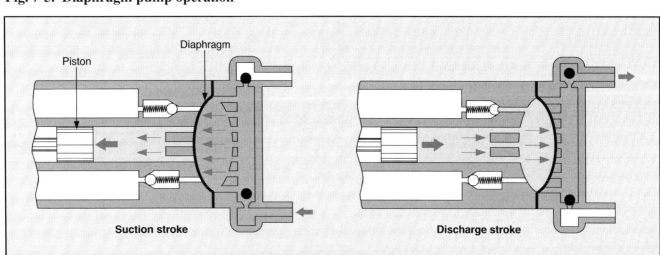

Fig. 7-6. Adjustable-stroke diaphragm pump

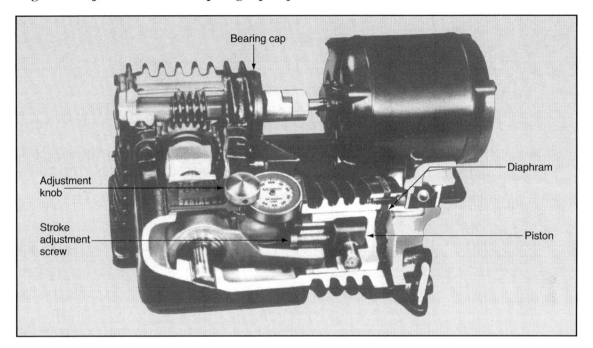

diaphragm flexes away from the fluid side. The vacuum produced in the cavity causes the discharge valve to close. The suction valve is forced open by the incoming fluid, and the pumped material is drawn into the open space.

7.28   The method of fluid control on the power side of the diaphragm varies with each manufacturer. However, the basic operation remains the same for all diaphragm pumps.

7.29   The power end of a diaphragm pump can be adjusted in one of several ways. One design uses an adjustable eccentric point between the crankshaft and the connecting rod of the plunger, in a manner similar to the adjustable-stroke plunger pump. By changing the stroke of the plunger in the power end, the amount of fluid forced against the diaphragm changes. This adjustment changes the amount of diaphragm movement and the amount of fluid pumped. Figure 7-6 shows an adjustable-stroke diaphragm pump.

7.30   Some manufacturers use a variable-speed drive connected to the pump plunger to control pump flow. The variable-speed drive changes the number of plunger strokes per minute instead of the length of the stroke.

7.31   Another manufacturer places the plunger directly within the crankshaft of the pump. The constant rotation of the crankshaft and plunger is converted to reciprocating motion by changing the position of the reaction ring, as shown in Fig. 7-7, on the following page.

Fig. 7-7. Diaphragm pump with rotating plunger

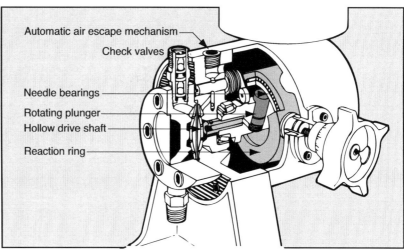

Shifting the reaction ring to one side or the other varies the amount of fluid that the plunger pumps as it rotates. The pulsating fluid is directed against the diaphragm, which flexes and pumps the fluid on the fluid side. This pump is designed to be adjustable while it is operating. Most mechanically adjustable pumps can be adjusted only when they are stopped.

7.32   A further variation of the basic diaphragm pump is shown in Fig. 7-8. As in other models, the piston on the power end of the diaphragm is driven by a crankshaft. The piston stroke is not usually adjustable. The amount of fluid pumped is regulated within the pump by means of a hydraulic fluid capacity adjusting knob. This knob varies the amount of

Fig. 7-8. Diaphragm pump with fluid capacity control

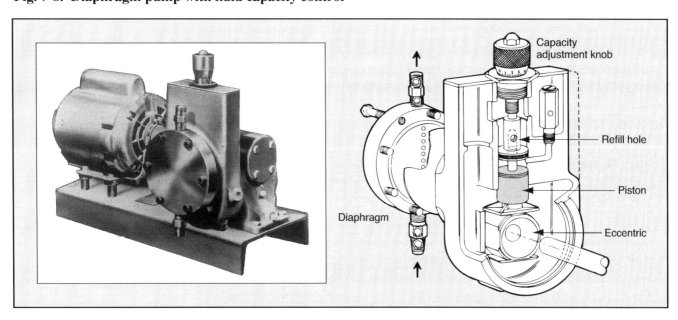

fluid admitted to the power side of the diaphragm by changing the position of the fluid-closing port.

7.33   Another type of diaphragm pump, which acts on the same principle, is shown in Fig. 7-9. In this particular pump, the diaphragm is cylindrical. Pumping takes place when the entire diaphragm cylinder flexes.

7.34   The cylindrical diaphragm is expanded by the hydraulic fluid pumped into the diaphragm interior. The amount of hydraulic fluid admitted to the diaphragm is regulated by a capacity-control port. As the plunger travels downward, control fluid is bypassed back to a reservoir until the control port is closed. The trapped fluid is then forced into the chamber, extending the diaphragm and pumping the fluid on the fluid side.

7.35   Stainless steel or another corrosion-resistant alloy usually forms the pump body. The diaphragm is made of a chemically resistant, flexible material. Most manufacturers make several diaphragms for each pump, each of a different material. Although these diaphragms are interchangeable, you must make sure that a particular diaphragm material is suitable for your particular application.

7.36   Both the suction and discharge valves are fluid-activated and are either of the ball or disk type. They may or may not be spring-loaded.

7.37   Most metering pumps that are mechanically adjustable by cams or varying speed arrangements can be controlled by electric or pneumatic

Fig. 7-9. Cylindrical-diaphragm pump

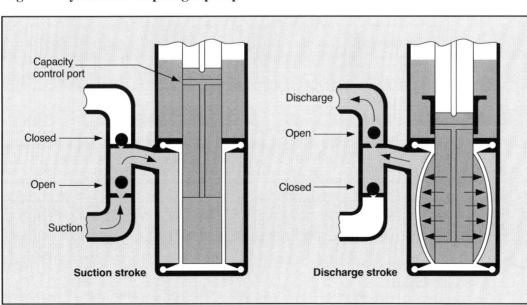

Fig. 7-10. Air-operated metering pump

actuating devices. These electric or pneumatic controls are connected to the adjustable metering control devices and can be remotely controlled.

7.38 Frequently, a sensing mechanism is inserted in the fluid-flow line to the main fluid system. In these applications, a pickup device will detect any variation in the makeup of the fluid. When it senses variation, it sends a signal to the controlling unit, which automatically makes a correction. For example, it might increase or decrease the amount of chemical being pumped.

Air-Operated Metering Pumps

7.39 An air-operated, reciprocating metering pump is shown in Fig. 7-10. The fluid end of the pump is similar in design, construction, and operation to those previously covered. The power end, however, is quite a bit different. Instead of using the rotary motion of a crankshaft or eccentric to create the reciprocating motion of the pump, an air cylinder is connected directly to the pump.

7.40 During operation, the air cylinder piston travel is controlled by limiting the amount of air admitted to the cylinder or by using a limit switch mounted on the connecting rod. Inlet air is usually controlled by an electrically timed metering device. This device automatically admits air to the cylinder at the required pressure and for a specific amount of time.

7.41 As the timer closes the inlet valve, the air that advances the piston in the air cylinder is shut off. Because the piston is in a sealed unit, however, the air that has been admitted remains there until the piston completes its stroke. In this way, the air holds the cylinder in position and allows the pump to make short, metered strokes instead of long, complete strokes.

7.42 As the piston reaches the end of its stroke, the air on the power side is vented, while air is admitted to the opposite side of the piston. This air movement reverses the air piston and returns it to its original position in one smooth movement. The power end of the diaphragm pump uses a spring-loaded diaphragm. In this case, the diaphragm is returned by spring action while the inlet air is vented to the atmosphere.

7.43 In air cylinders that use a limit switch as the control mechanism, the actuating air is stopped and started somewhat differently. As the trip mechanisms attached to the connecting rod pass a limit switch, the air inlet valve opens or closes as required. When the cylinder reaches the end of its stroke, the air is vented. Air is admitted to the opposite side, and the piston returns to its starting position. During its return stroke, a limit-switch override is used to prevent the limit switches from stopping the smooth return movement of the cylinder.

7.44   The return of the piston to its original position draws fluid into the pump chamber. This is true of all metering pumps that use pistons or plungers. As in other pump models, fluid intake and discharge are controlled and directed by a set of check valves.

Rotary Metering Pumps

7.45   Rotary metering pumps are most often vane pumps. Their construction is similar to that of the fixed-capacity vane pump covered in Chapter Five. In order for the pump to have a variable flow, however, the body housing is made movable about a central point.

7.46   This arrangement is shown in Fig. 7-11. The outer body of the pump can be rotated clockwise or counterclockwise to vary the amount of fluid pumped. Changing the position of the body changes its position with

Fig. 7-11. Vane metering pump operation

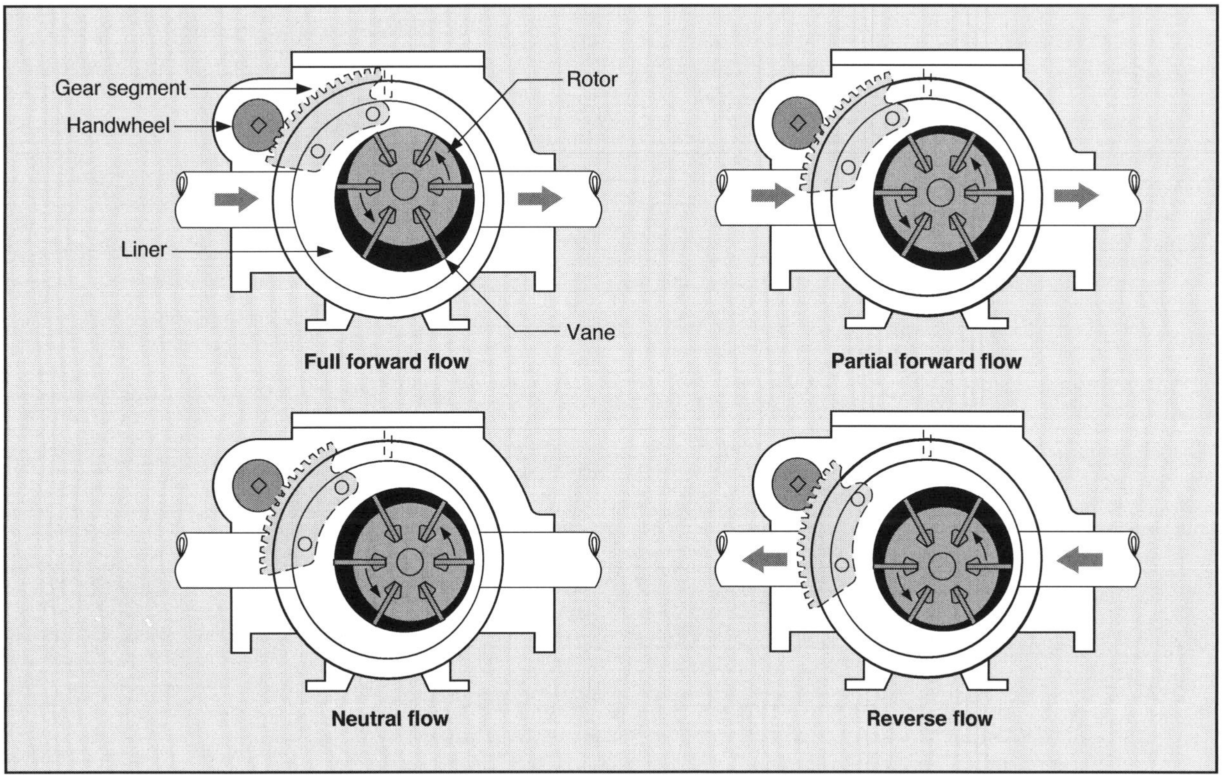

Fig. 7-12. External gear metering pump

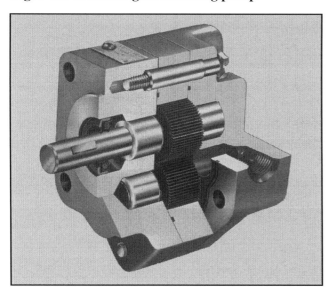

respect to the impeller vanes. With this arrangement, fluid delivery can be varied to suit the conditions at hand.

7.47   The position of the pump body is changed by turning a handwheel mounted on the outside of the pump. This handwheel rotates the worm on the other end of the shaft. The worm changes the position of the gear segment, which is connected to the pump body.

7.48   Another rotary pump design sometimes used for metering is the gear pump. It becomes a metering pump when driven by a variable-speed motor. On some internal gear models, the crescent segment is movable. Moving the crescent changes the position of the idler gear with respect to the inlet opening in the pump body. This adjustment reverses the fluid direction. No changes are necessary in the piping or valves. External-gear pumps, like the one shown in Fig. 7-12, are also used for metering.

7.49   *Peristaltic pumps* (flexible tube or liner pumps) are also sometimes used for metering purposes. Variable-speed motors allow precise control.

7.50   The materials used in the construction of rotary metering pumps depends upon the application for which the pump is used. Like most other metering pumps, the pump body, impeller, and internal pump housing are made of materials that are corrosion-resistant. The materials are selected for long service life with little maintenance.

Chapter Eight

Special-Purpose Pumps

Handling Difficult Materials

8.01   Chapter One discussed several systems used to pump difficult materials. This chapter provides more examples, plus detailed information about the design, construction, and operation of the pumps used.

8.02   The term *difficult material* can have different meanings for different people. In one plant, a difficult material might be an extremely corrosive chemical. In another plant, it might be a semi-solid or abrasive material. Your plant probably has its own kinds of difficult materials.

8.03   Some materials are problems under certain conditions but not under others. Oil, for example, is difficult to pump in the crude stages. After it is refined, however, it becomes an easy material to pump. The remainder of this chapter will cover some common difficult-material applications and special-purpose pumps.

Chemical Pumps

8.04   Because of the increase in the use of chemical products in recent years, chemical pumps are more commonly used in all industries. The chemicals pumped might be hot, corrosive, viscous, or difficult in other ways. Commonly pumped chemical materials also include liquid fertilizer, acid, solvent, and plastic resin.

8.05   Most plastic products start out as liquid chemicals. These liquids are sometimes called *resins*. These resins often must be piped throughout the chemical plant before they are ready for conversion to the final product. During final processing, the resins might be converted to dry pellets or powder, or they might remain in liquid form.

8.06   Often the resins are combined with another chemical agent, called a *catalyst,* during final mixing. The catalyst causes a chemical reaction in the resin that causes it to harden. Fiberglass products use resin as a base during the manufacturing process.

8.07   Pumps used to handle resins are usually air-operated reciprocating pumps. Reciprocating pumps are used because the resins have a high viscosity, requiring a positive-displacement pump to move them. The stalling characteristic of the air-operated pump maintains constant pressure throughout the system, even when the fluid is not being pumped. In addition, the straight-line motion of the piston reduces heat buildup and foaming, problems frequently caused by rotary pumps.

8.08   Less viscous chemicals are usually handled by centrifugal pumps like the ones shown in Fig. 8-1. The first consideration when selecting a chemical pump is to make sure the materials used for both the pump casing and the impeller can resist attack by the chemical being pumped. The proper corrosion-resistant seals must also be selected.

8.09   Many pump casings are made of corrosion- resistant alloys. Others are made of Teflon®, polypropolyene, chlorinated polyvinyl chloride (CPVC), and similar materials. Most materials can be used with more than one chemical. However, you must take care to ensure that the materials selected

®Teflon is a registered trademark of the E. I. du Pont de Nemours & Co., Inc.

Fig. 8-1. Chemical pumps

for a chemical pumping system are compatible with the fluid and will not corrode or erode because of the chemical action within the system.

8.10   A special centrifugal chemical pump is shown in Fig. 8-2. Although the pump resembles a common end-suction centrifugal pump, it differs in construction. The entire casing, impeller, and shaft sleeve are made of impervious graphite. Use of the graphite material results in a pump that is strong, lightweight, and highly resistant to acids and salt solutions. In addition, the pump shown is available with silicon-carbide treated parts for use with abrasive and corrosive fluids.

Special Chemical Pumps

8.11   Some unusual kinds of pumps are sometimes used in chemical pumping applications. These pumps are also good to use when pumping viscous fluids or thick slurries.

8.12   The pump shown in Fig. 8-3 is called a *flexible-tube pump* or *peristaltic pump*. This type of pump was covered briefly in Chapter Five. As the pump rollers come into contact with the flexible tube, they press the pumping tube against a curved track. As the roller travels through its circle, the tube is compressed, forcing any fluid ahead of the roller out the discharge port. After the roller passes, the tube returns to its original shape and draws in fluid from the intake side.

8.13   Peristaltic pumps are available with different numbers of rollers to change their capacity. The tubes are usually made of natural or synthetic rubbers. The compression tubes must be not only flexible, but also elastic in order to resume their shape after they have been compressed. Tubing comes in many diameters and wall thicknesses. The larger the tube diameter, the greater the capacity of the pump. Peristaltic pump capacities range from 5 to 2000 gph.

8.14   Figure 8-4, on the following page, shows a *flexible-liner pump*. This pump was covered

Fig. 8-2. Graphite pump

Fig. 8-3. Flexible-tube pump

Fig. 8-4. Flexible-liner pump

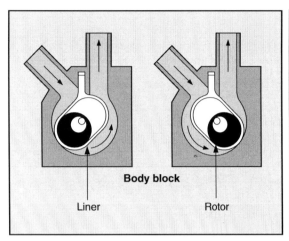

briefly in Chapter Five. Because it is sealless and has few moving parts, it can handle corrosives, volatile fluids, and abrasives safely and efficiently.

8.15   As shown in Fig. 8-4, a rotor mounted on an eccentric shaft oscillates within the liner, thus creating a progressive squeegee action on the fluid trapped between the liner and the body block. The pumped fluid contacts only the outer surface of the liner and the inner surface of the body block. These surfaces may be made of various plastics, natural or synthetic rubbers, stainless steel, or other materials.

8.16   A *progressing-cavity pump* is shown in Fig. 8-5. This pump, which is sometimes referred to as a *single-screw pump,* was also covered briefly

Fig. 8-5. Progressing-cavity pumps

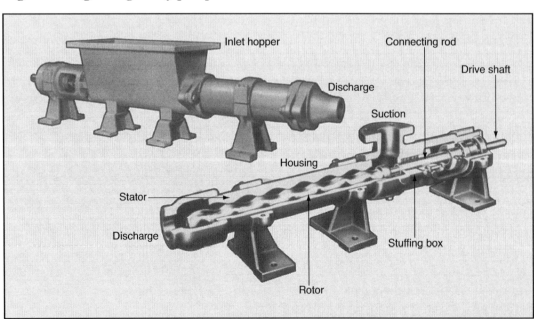

in Chapter Five. This pump is actually a positive-displacement rotary screw pump. Because of its construction, it is particularly suitable for pumping viscous solutions and thick slurries.

8.17   This pump is composed of five main parts—the housing, the stator, the rotor, the connecting rod, and the drive shaft. The rotor is usually made of either chrome-plated tool steel or stainless steel. The stator is made from natural rubber, Buna-N, butyl rubber, or other materials. The material selected for the rotor and stator is determined by the application.

8.18   In operation, the fluid enters at the suction end of the pump and flows into the open cavity between the rotor and the stator. As the pump rotates, the fluid is forced along the open area in the stator. Continued rotation of the rotor forces the fluid toward the discharge port.

8.19   Figure 8-5 shows the stuffing box on the drive shaft. The connecting rod is located within the drive shaft. Because the connecting rod dead-ends within the drive shaft, it will not allow any fluid leakage. The only place leakage can occur is through the stuffing box. Because the fluid flows away from the stuffing box, the packing is in a negative pressure area, except when the pump is stopped.

8.20   The progressing-cavity pump can be operated in reverse. When operating in reverse, the fluid flow and rotor action can remove any plugging in the suction or discharge line, or in the pump itself. After the obstruction is removed, reversing the pump again restores it to its original rotation, allowing regular pumping to resume.

8.21   The pump housing is usually made of cast iron, but cast steel or cast stainless steel are also used. The housing can be either of one or two-piece construction, depending upon the size of the pump.

8.22   Progressing-cavity pumps are frequently used in food processing plants and refineries, as well as in chemical plants. These pumps are also used to handle sewage and industrial waste. The temperature of the pumped fluid should be kept below 200°F to keep the stator from drying out and becoming brittle.

8.23   Progressing-cavity pumps can even be used for pumping mineral gypsum, perlite, and other roof materials. In these applications, the inlet pipe is replaced by an inlet hopper with a rectangular opening or throat. The rectangular opening prevents the material from bridging. A small screw conveyor or feeder at the bottom of the hopper ensures full material flow to the pump rotor. This design is also shown in Fig. 8-5.

Fig. 8-6. Magnetic-drive pump

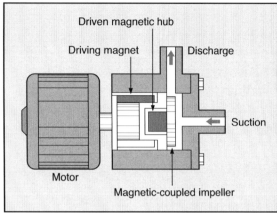

Magnetic-Drive Pumps

8.24   Although many improvements have made pumps increasingly resistant to chemical attack, one problem remains. That problem is leakage. Although many types of sealing devices have been used with good results, better sealing methods are always being sought. As a result, the sealless *magnetic-drive pump* was perfected. This pump is shown in Fig. 8-6.

8.25   From the outside, the magnetic-drive pump looks like many other chemical pumps. Its construction, however, is very different from that of other centrifugal pumps.

8.26   The impeller of the magnetic-drive pump has an extension hub on its driving side that extends into the pump housing, as shown in Fig. 8-6. The impeller hub is made of a magnetic material. When the pump is operating, the motor drives a small circular magnet located at the rear of the pump housing. The magnet is positioned around the impeller hub and controls both the impeller's speed and position. As the motor turns the driving magnet, magnetic flux passes through the pump housing and couples the rotation of the motor and impeller.

8.27   There are two things to remember when using pumps of this type. First, the pump is not designed to operate under suction lift conditions. It must have a positive suction head and must be primed (filled with fluid) before it is started. Second, because the impeller hub is magnetic, it can wander during operation. The positioning and balancing of the impeller hub are aided by the fluid passing through the pump.

Fig. 8-7. Canned-motor pump

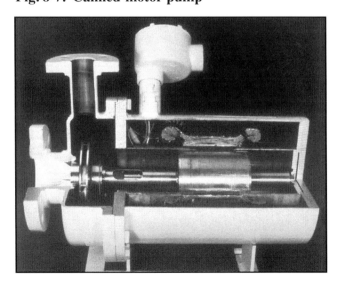

8.28   Because of their characteristics, magnetic-drive pumps are usually made for fixed-capacity applications. Most of these pumps operate with small motors and handle flows from about 0.5 to 25 gpm.

Canned-Motor Pumps

8.29   *Canned-motor pumps* are sealless, close-coupled, centrifugal pumps, with the motor and pump contained in a common sealed steel enclosure or can. Motor bearings run in the pumped fluid, thus eliminating the need for shaft seals. Since the pumped fluid is also the lubricant, it is important that no solid particles or grit enter the pump. A typical canned-motor pump is pictured in Fig. 8-7.

8.30   Single-stage canned-motor pumps are available for deliveries up to 700 gpm at heads up to 250 ft. Two-stage pumps will deliver heads up to 600 ft. Canned-motor pumps are commonly used to pump liquid refrigerants, solvents, heat-transfer fluids, and light oils. They are also well suited for applications involving toxic or hazardous liquids, where no leakage can be tolerated.

Centrifugal Slurry Pumps

8.31   The slurry pumps used in industry can handle a wide variety of materials. Because many of the materials are abrasive, the pump is expected to wear. For this reason, pumps are often modular in design and have renewable segments for easier maintenance and accessibility. An example of a modular slurry pump is shown in Fig. 8-8. When

Fig. 8-8. Modular slurry pump

Fig. 8-9. Lined slurry pump

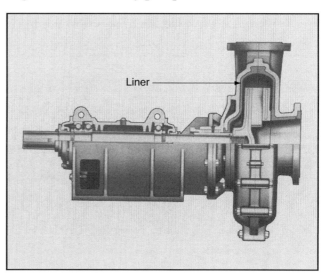

using this type of pump, you can remove and replace parts easily and quickly.

8.32   Most slurry pumps are centrifugal pumps. Some are diaphragm pumps, which will be discussed later in this chapter.

8.33   Many slurry pumps are lined with rubber, ceramic, or other abrasion-resistant materials. An example of a lined pump is shown in Fig. 8-9, on the previous page.

8.34   Some slurry pumps use semi-open impellers, while others use closed impellers. Slurry-pump impellers are usually relatively large and have only a few widely spaced vanes. This allows the slurry to pass through without clogging the impeller.

8.35   Because the materials handled by slurry pumps are bulky and viscous, large-horsepower motors are required. Many of these pumps are mounted on bedplates that support not only the motors, but also speed-reducing devices.

Pulp-Handling Pumps

8.36   Centrifugal pulp-handling pumps are commonly used in paper mills. Impellers are usually open, as shown in Fig. 8-10, although closed impellers are sometimes used.

8.37   As in other slurry pumps, the impellers of these pumps are fairly large in diameter and have only a few vanes. Some pumps used for pulp are connected to a screw conveyor or other feeding mechanism. The grabbing action of the screw conveyor or feeder breaks up the pulp and draws it into the pump.

Fig. 8-10. Pulp-handling pump

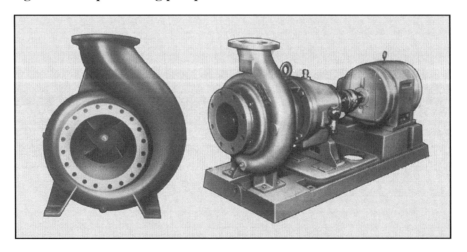

Trash and Sewage Pumps

Fig. 8-11. Sump pumps

8.38   Trash and sewage pumps, like slurry pumps, must move a certain amount of debris. Usually, they are of the wet-sump design and are placed directly in the fluid being pumped. Sometimes these pumps are used to pump out excavations or flooded areas. These pumps must be able to handle trash, twigs, rags, and stone.

8.39   The centrifugal pumps shown in Fig. 8-11 are examples of those used for wet-sump applications. The impeller and the pump casing are fairly large, which allows the bulky materials to pass without clogging the pump. These pumps usually have their suction intake on the underside.

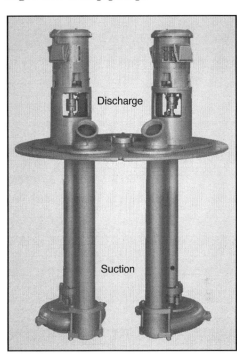

8.40   Note that on the dry-type sump pump shown in Fig. 8-12, the suction intake is near the top. By having the suction intake above the impeller, a small amount of fluid is retained within the pump casing when the pump stops. This feature makes the pump self-priming. If the pump has never been used, pour a small amount of water into the top of the pump to prime it. Once

Fig. 8-12. Dry-type sump pump

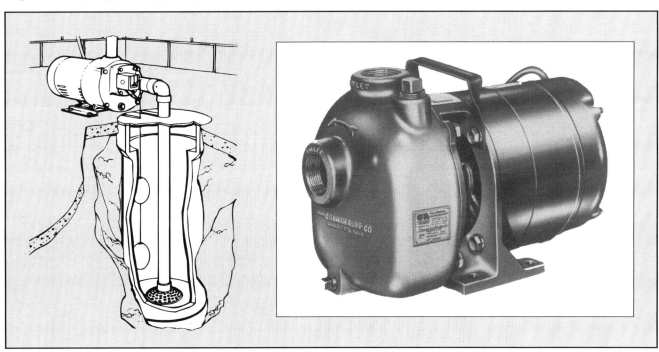

the pump has been used, it will normally retain its prime unless the water is drained out completely.

8.41   On portable sump pumps, the section of the pump just ahead of the impeller is usually removable. Also, a small cover plate in front of the impeller is provided to allow you to clean out debris that collects on the suction side. Although not all pumps are exactly the same, most sump pumps are made with easy access for cleaning.

8.42   Some pumps have guide vanes attached to the cover to direct the flow of material into the impeller. To increase pump life, a wearplate or liner can be bolted to the cover. The impellers are usually of the semi-open type.

Diaphragm Pumps

8.43   Although diaphragm pumps are often thought of as metering pumps, they can also be used for transferring fluids, slurries, or sewage. The pumping action of diaphragm pumps is similar to the pumping action of other types of reciprocating pumps.

8.44   Diaphragm pumps operate with a flexing action. The diaphragm can be deflected mechanically or by hydraulic or air pressure. The mechanically displaced design requires a pressure-relief valve. The air and hydraulic designs, because of their stalling characteristic, do not require relief valves.

8.45   Diaphragms can be made of metal or inert plastic. The diaphragm's only function is to isolate the pumped fluid from the motivating force. When used to pump chemicals or other corrosive fluids, diaphragm pumps should either be lined or manufactured of stainless steel or other corrosion-resistant materials.

8.46   Mechanically actuated pumps are commonly used for low-pressure service. An unsupported diaphragm is moved in the discharge direction by an eccentric cam and is returned by a compression spring.

8.47   Air-operated double-diaphragm pumps, like the ones shown in Fig. 8-13, have two flexible diaphragms connected by a common shaft. As compressed air is admitted behind one diaphragm, the air behind the other is exhausted. At the end of a stroke, air flow is automatically reversed by an air distribution valve. One pumping chamber is always filling while the other is discharging. This simultaneous intake/discharge pumping action is illustrated in Fig. 8-14.

Fig. 8-13. Air-operated double-diaphragm pumps

Reciprocating Slurry Pumps

8.48   In addition to diaphragm slurry pumps, two other types of reciprocating slurry pumps are available. Both are shown in Fig. 8-15, on the following page. The air- or steam-operated pump is a close relative of other direct-acting reciprocating pumps of the side-pot design. The air- or steam-driven reciprocating slurry pump usually has renewable cylinder sleeves and valve seats. These are the parts that receive the most wear and, therefore, require the most

Fig. 8-14. Fluid action in a diaphragm pump

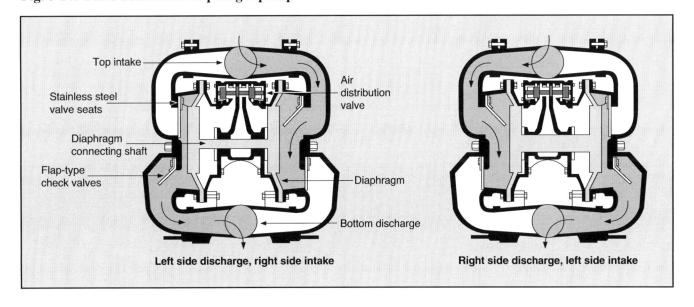

Fig. 8-15. Reciprocating slurry pumps

maintenance. To ensure long operating life, the pump must be equipped with renewable parts.

8.49   The other type of reciprocating slurry pump shown is motor or engine driven. In this type of pump, the fluid end is similar to the one in the air- or steam-operated slurry pump. The power end, however, is driven by a crankshaft through a connecting rod. A separate cylinder rod guide or crosshead provides the flexible point needed to connect the piston rod to the connecting rod.

Fig. 8-16. Vortex pump

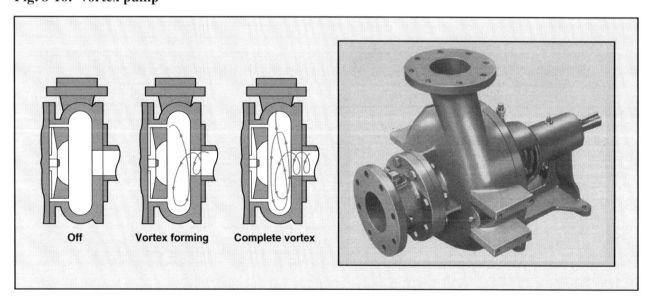

8.50   The check valves of these slurry pumps can be rubber lined or can be made entirely of molded rubber. The use of rubber in the valves reduces valve wear when abrasive materials are pumped. Note that these pumps are of the double-acting type, which means they will maintain a constant flow of fluid with only a slight pulsation as the piston reaches the end of the stroke.

Vortex Pumps

8.51   Vortex pumps are often used to pump sewage, slurries, and other fluids with a high solids content. They are also useful for pumping fluids containing large amounts of air and gas. These pumps have capacities to about 1200 gpm and produce discharge heads to 180 ft. Figure 8-16 shows a vortex pump.

8.52   The impeller of the vortex pump is placed in such a way that no more than half its depth extends into the pump case. In some cases, the impeller is completely behind the case. This placement allows an unobstructed flow of fluid with almost no interference by the impeller.

8.53   Because of the impeller location, pumped particles need not pass through the blades of the impeller. The vortex is formed in front of the blades. Nearly any material that will pass through the suction piping will pass through the pump and out the discharge. The food industry pumps beans, cherries, peas, and even live fish with this type of pump.

8.54   As in a typical end-suction centrifugal pump, the impeller transfers mechanical energy to the pumped fluid. The fluid is not thrown against the inside of the pump case, however, because the impeller is not within the case. The water twists and moves out of the discharge, causing a partial vacuum at the center of the impeller.

8.55   The partial vacuum, along with the vortex action of the fluid, pulls fluid up the suction line. As fluid enters the vortex within the pump housing, it is thrown by centrifugal force to the outer edge of the pump case. It then twirls around until it exits through the discharge. Typical fluid flow is also illustrated in Fig. 8-16.

8.56   Vortex pumps can be frame mounted vertically or horizontally or can be obtained as submersible pumps. Unlike the volute case of an end-suction pump, the case of the vortex pump is nearly round. This feature allows the vortex pump to hold its prime more readily, since there is no area in the case in which air can become trapped.

Chapter Nine

Packings and Seals

9

Pump Sealing Requirements

9.01   In pumps, the impellers and pistons that impart motion to the fluid being pumped are always driven by a shaft. To prevent fluid leakage along the driving shaft, sealing devices are used. Shaft sealing devices must control fluid leakage without causing wear to the pump shaft. If shaft wear occurs, an expensive and time-consuming shaft replacement job must be performed.

9.02   Although shaft seals are designed to control fluid leakage from the pump, a slight amount of leakage through the seals on most pumps is required. This leakage lubricates the shaft and the seal and cools the contacting surfaces.

9.03   Some pumps have a supply line connected to the seal area. This line directs fluid to the packing to cool and lubricate it. The cooling fluid might be the fluid being pumped. If the pumped fluid is hot, corrosive, or abrasive, the fluid is supplied from an outside source.

9.04   The first half of this chapter covers stuffing boxes. The second half covers mechanical seals. *Stuffing boxes* are sealing areas that are manually packed and adjusted. They contain braided cotton, Teflon®, carbon, graphite, or synthetic sealing materials. *Mechanical seals* are molded seals held in place by springs or other constant-pressure devices.

Stuffing Boxes

9.05   Small pumps with a single shaft entrance generally use only one stuffing box. Many pumps, however, use a through shaft supported by externally mounted bearings. Small pumps have two stuffing boxes, one on either side of the casing.

9.06   When installing a new pump, always check the stuffing box for packing. Some pumps are shipped with the stuffing boxes packed, and some are not. If the boxes are packed, the packing is usually loose and must be adjusted or tightened both before the pump is filled with fluid and again after start-up.

9.07   Before starting the pump, it is a good idea to make sure that the stuffing boxes allow a slight amount of leakage. However, once the pump is running, the amount of leakage should be reduced to a minimum to prevent fluid damage to surrounding equipment.

Types of Stuffing Boxes

9.08   Several kinds of stuffing boxes are used in industrial pumps. The kind used in a particular pump depends upon the application, the design of the pump, and the pump manufacturer.

9.09   The most common stuffing box arrangement used in pumps is the *solid-packed stuffing box,* as shown in Fig. 9-1. In this arrangement, the pump casing has a retaining ridge or lip at the interior edge of the pump. (The interior edge is the one closest to the fluid being pumped.) Many pump manufacturers equip the pump shaft with a replacement sleeve. This sleeve protects the shaft from wear by the packing, thereby reducing maintenance repair costs and lost time.

9.10   *A packing gland* is placed on the outer end of the packing rings. As the packing rings wear and leakage increases, you can adjust the gland to reduce the amount of leakage. Because a solid-packed stuffing box has no built-in means of lubrication, you must not draw the packing down too tightly. A small amount of leakage is necessary to cool and lubricate the shaft and packing.

9.11   Pumps that are supplied with this simple stuffing box should not be used under suction lift conditions. When used under such conditions, air can be drawn in through the packing. This causes the pump to become airbound or to lose fluid suction.

9.12   Pumps designed to operate under suction lift conditions use a sealing or *injection-type*

Fig. 9-1. Solid-packed stuffing box

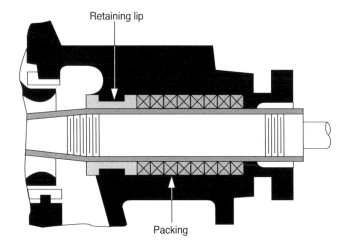

Retaining lip

Packing

109

Fig. 9-2. Injection-type stuffing boxes

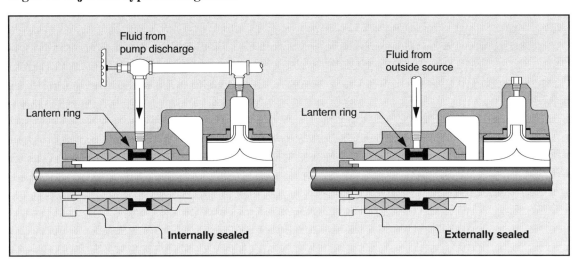

stuffing box. This arrangement uses fluid to help seal the packing and keep air from being drawn in. The fluid can come from the discharge side of the pump or from another source, as shown in Fig. 9-2. If the sealing fluid is supplied by the pump, the pump is said to be *internally sealed.* If the sealing fluid is supplied from a source outside the pump, it is *externally sealed.* Some pumps have provisions for both internal and external sealing, and either can be used as needed.

9.13   When a pump uses an injection-type stuffing box, some means must be provided to distribute the sealing fluid within the box. Usually this is done with a lantern ring. *Lantern rings* are commonly made of brass or plastic and separate the packing into two sections. Rings must be correctly positioned in the pump to distribute the sealing liquid properly along the shaft. Figure 9-3 shows a lantern ring.

9.14   If a pump is to handle gritty or corrosive fluids, the sealing fluid must be obtained from an outside source. In addition, the sealing fluid should be at a higher pressure than the pump suction pressure. If the pump is to handle gasoline, kerosene, oil, or similar materials, it is especially important that the sealing fluid be compatible with the fluid being pumped.

9.15   A variation of the injection-type stuffing box is shown in Fig. 9-4, on the following page. This arrangement is called a *circulating stuffing box system.* In this system, the sealing fluid enters on one side of the stuffing box (usually the top). It passes through the sealing area and is

Fig. 9-3. Lantern ring

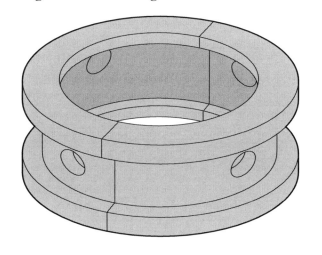

Fig. 9-4. Circulating stuffing box system

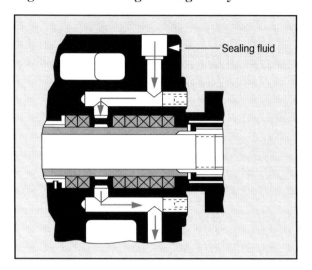

discharged through an opening on the opposite side of the pump casing.

9.16   The sealing fluid performs two functions as it flows along the stuffing box. First, it seals the pumped fluid within the pump. Second, the circulating fluid cools the packing and the shaft or sleeve. This arrangement is especially useful if the pumped fluid is hot. Supplying cooling water to the packing keeps it cool, thus extending its life.

9.17   Another kind of stuffing box arrangement is the *bleed-off system,* as shown in Fig. 9-5. In this system, a small amount of the fluid being pumped is internally discharged by the pump into the throat bushing of the stuffing box. The fluid drain is called the *bleed-off point.* It is usually connected to the suction side of the system, so the fluid is not discharged as waste material.

9.18   In the bleed-off system, sealing fluid can be injected into the portion of the pump casing just ahead of the stuffing box, as shown in Fig. 9-6. In this injection/bleed-off system, the bled-off fluid is handled as waste.

9.19   Pumps handling fluids that can form flammable gases or noxious fumes use a *smothering* or *quench system.* The smothering system is similar to the injection bleed-off system just described, but is positioned at the exterior end of the stuffing box. By locating the sealing fluid entrance at this point, noxious gases or vapors that escape past the packing rings

Fig. 9-5. Bleed-off stuffing box system

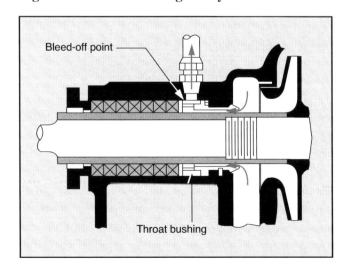

Fig. 9-6. Combination injection/bleed-off system

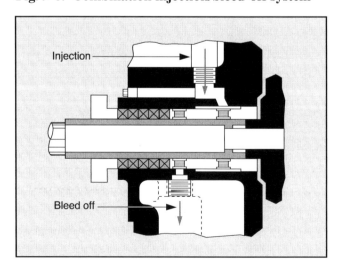

are trapped by the cooling water and reduced to a nonhazardous state. The discharge from a smothering system is usually treated as waste.

Packing Materials

9.20   The materials commonly used to make packing include cotton, flax, Teflon, carbon, graphite, and, most recently, various synthetic materials. Usually these materials are woven or braided to form a continuous strand. The strands are sometimes wire reinforced and usually have some type of coating. The coating acts as a lubricant and also as a bonding agent to help the packing retain its shape. Several styles of packing are shown in Fig. 9-7, on the following page.

9.21   Packing can be purchased in long strands on spools, or it can be purchased precut to a specified size. If the packing is purchased as a long strand, it must be cut to size in the plant as required. When the packing rings are precut, they are often packaged in quantities sufficient to repack an entire stuffing box. They might even be in the form of preformed rings.

9.22   Flax and cotton packing materials are most commonly used on pumps that handle cool liquids. Pumps that handle liquids over 220°F (105°C) are usually packed with Teflon or synthetic, carbon, or graphitic materials.

9.23   Petroleum pumps, which have operating temperatures around 450°F (230°C), usually use packing materials made of aluminum or babbitt. These metallic packings are made in the form of crinkled foil or folded ribbon, with or without a core. Because of its low melting point, babbitt is used for temperatures below 450°F. Aluminum foil is used for pumps having temperatures over 450°F. Recently, carbon and graphitic packings have been introduced for use on petroleum pumps. These materials exhibit excellent heat and chemical resistance. Table 9-1, on the following page, gives more information on packing materials recommended for various applications.

Installing Packing

9.24   It is extremely important that you use the proper methods when you repack a pump. Incorrect packing installation causes many packing failures and much pump damage. As a general rule, you should replace packing when leakage cannot be controlled by tightening the packing gland. The following paragraphs outline the correct way to install pump packing.

Fig. 9-7. Packing styles

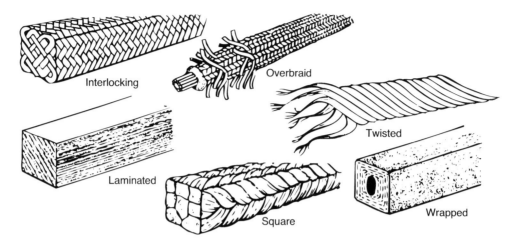

Interlocking

Overbraid

Twisted

Laminated

Square

Wrapped

9.25   First, make sure you shut off and lock out power to the pump. Remove all the old packing from the stuffing box. Clean the box and the shaft and examine the shaft or sleeve for wear or scoring. If wear is excessive, replace the shaft or sleeve.

9.26   To find the correct packing size, measure the diameter of the shaft, then the diameter of the stuffing box. If the shaft is worn, be sure to make the shaft measurement within the stuffing box area. Subtract the shaft measurement from the stuffing box measurement, then divide by two. The answer will give you the correct packing size.

9.27   If you are working with a continuous strand of packing, you should cut the packing into rings. Never wind the strand into the stuffing

Table 9-1. Packing recommendations

Fluid	Packing	Fluid	Packing
Clear water (hot or cold), sewage slurries, calcium brine, neutral liquids. Maximum temperature—212°F (100°C).	Flax or cotton, plaited construction with general service lubricant. Graphited.	Solvents, alcohols, chlorinated hydrocarbons, fuel oils, kerosene. Maximum temperature—250°F (120°C).	Teflon, TFE, and impregnated synthetics.
Clear water (hot or cold), neutral liquids. Maximum temperature—400°F (205°C).	Synthetics or Teflon, plaited construction with a high-temperature lubricant. Graphited.	Where metallic packing is preferred for cold or hot water, mild alkalies, mild acids, brine, boiler feed service. Maximum temperature—450°F (230°C). Where suction pressure exceeds 50 psi.	Crinkled lead foil sheets with resilient core.
Acids (sulfuric, nitric, and others). Maximum temperature—250°F (120°C).	Teflon, carbon, graphite, or synthetics, plaited construction with an acid-resisting lubricant.	Alkalies and other liquids with pH factors above 7. For temperatures of 90 to 450°F (32 to 230°C).	Teflon, synthetics, carbon, or graphite.
Alkalies (caustic soda, silicate of soda, sulphates, Kraft liquors, salt brine, and others). Maximum temperature—250°F (120°C).	Same as above.	Acids, weak or concentrated, specifically those with a pH factor of 4 or less. For temperature of 90 to 450°F (32 to 230°C).	Same as above.
Food products, beverages, and other applications where non-contamination is the governing factor. Maximum temperature—180°F (80°C).	Teflon and Teflon-impregnated synthetics		

box. Hold the packing tightly on the shaft, but do not stretch it excessively. You can cut rings with butt, bias, or diagonal joints.

9.28 You can cut each ring by winding the packing around the shaft, or you can use the first ring as a master from which to cut the rest of the rings. If the rings are not cut to the correct size, packing life will be greatly reduced.

9.29 Precut rings can be a great advantage because they give you the exact ring size for the diameters of the shaft and stuffing box. There is no waste and no worry about incorrect fit.

9.30 Before installing a ring, make sure that it has not picked up any dirt. Install one ring at a time, making certain that it fits properly. Then seat each ring firmly (unless the packing manufacturer suggests otherwise). Stagger the joints of the rings so that they are about 90° apart. Seat each ring with a tamping tool as it is installed.

9.31 After the last ring has been installed, replace the packing gland and adjust it evenly. Do not jam the packing into place by over-tightening the gland. Start the pump and allow it to leak freely for 15 min. Then tighten the gland gradually until leakage is decreased to a tolerable minimum. Make sure to take up gland bolts evenly. Do not stop leakage entirely at this point, or the packing will burn up.

9.32 If the stuffing box has a lantern ring, make sure that it is installed slightly behind the sealing fluid inlet so that it will move under the inlet when the gland is tightened.

Mechanical Seals

9.33 Mechanical seals are used in many pumps to prevent fluid leakage. Mechanical seals might be chosen over packing on a given application for two reasons. First, mechanical seals provide a better fluid seal than packing. Second, mechanical seals usually require less maintenance than packing. This fact is especially advantageous if the pump is in an out-of-the-way place. Third, mechanical seals can withstand higher pressures than stuffing boxes.

9.34 Many different types of mechanical seals are available, and pump manufacturers have preferences for mounting seals in their pumps. All seals have similar components and operate in a similar manner. For special applications, some pump manufacturers design their own seals. Even though they are custom-made, these seals function in the same manner as other mechanical seals.

Fig. 9-8. Typical mechanical seal

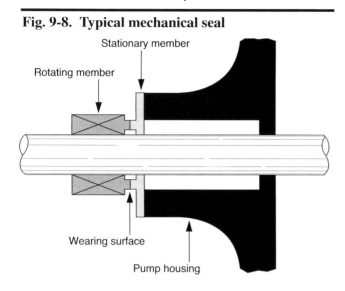

9.35   Nearly all mechanical seals consist of two main parts—a *rotating member* and a *stationary member*—as shown in Fig. 9-8. The illustration shows the relationship between the parts of the seal and the pump. More details on the seals themselves are given later in this chapter.

9.36   The contacting or wearing surfaces of the two parts are highly polished. This fine finish is important if the surfaces are to seal properly. To ensure proper contact between the parts, the shaft or pump housing on which they are mounted must be free of burrs and other surface irregularities. The seal and shaft must also be of compatible materials to prevent corrosion of the shaft and seal parts. Corrosion at this point can prevent the seal from moving or flexing with the shaft, thus breaking the seal between the two members.

9.37   Mechanical seals can be classified as *cartridge seals* and *separate seals*. They are similar in operation but differ in construction. Cartridge and separate seals are shown in Fig. 9-9.

9.38   The cartridge seal has a metal housing that encloses all of the component parts except the stationary member. The stationary member is held by the pump housing. A spring holds the rotating member in contact with the stationary member. The spring can be one large coil that fits over the shaft or several small coils spaced around the circumference of the shaft.

Fig. 9-9. Cartridge and separate mechanical seals

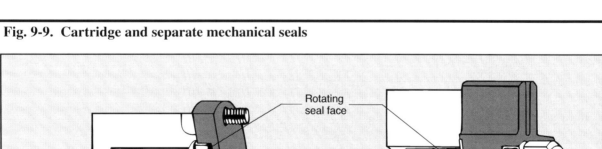

9.39   Mechanical seals are also classified according to the way they are installed and operated. They are classified in this way as *internal seals* and *external seals.* As shown in Fig. 9-10, an internal seal's rotating member is mounted within the seal housing near the fluid end of the pump. The stationary member is located outside. On the external seal, the stationary member is located toward the fluid side of the pump, and the rotating member is mounted outside the pump housing. Both of these seals are single seals, which means that only one sealing element is used. Most mechanically sealed pumps use single seals.

9.40   Occasionally, pumps use double seals similar to the one shown in Fig. 9-11, on the following page. In this application, the seals are mounted back-to-back with the stationary members at the outer extremities of the packing area. One stationary member is located at the inner edge of the stuffing box, near the fluid. The other member is located at the outer edge of the box.

9.41   Many industrial pumps use variations of these basic seal arrangements. These variations include gland cooling, lubrication, flushing, and venting. These variations have little effect on the configuration of the seal itself. Most of the changes are made in the seal housing.

9.42   Mechanical seals are also classified as *balanced* or *unbalanced.* This classification does not refer to the static or dynamic balance of the seal itself, but to the method by which internal pressure is applied to the seal face.

9.43   An unbalanced seal is shown in Fig. 9-12, on the following page. The pressure of the fluid within the pump housing and the mechanical pressure applied by the seal spring act on the rear portion of the seal's rotating member. This pressure forces it against the stationary member. A slight amount of force from the fluid being pumped tries to push the

Fig. 9-10. Internal and external seals

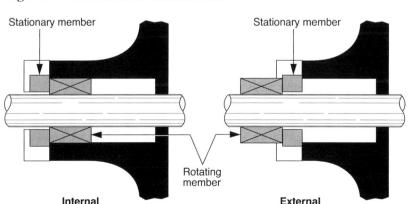

Fig. 9-11. Double mechanical seal

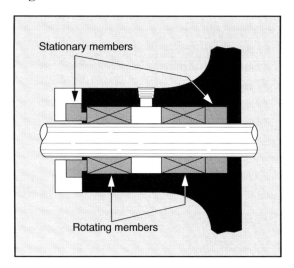

Fig. 9-12. Unbalanced seal

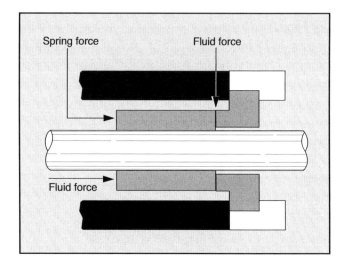

rotating and stationary members apart. But because this force acts perpendicularly to the other forces, it is less than the applied end force.

9.44   In a balanced seal design, the mechanical seal also has fluid forces and mechanical forces acting on it from within the pump housing, as shown in Fig. 9-13. Note, however, that the seal's rotating member has a step design on its front edge. This step allows a certain amount of pumped fluid to counteract the force on the back of the seal element. This force relieves some of the pressure on the seal, thus producing lighter contact pressure between the rotating and stationary elements. This lighter contact pressure increases seal life and ensures adequate lubrication of the contacting surfaces.

9.45   On mechanical seals, a secondary seal is needed between the shaft and the rotating seal member. Usually, wedge or O-ring seals are used. Internal fluid pressure or spring pressure provide the necessary force to maintain contact between the seal component and the shaft.

Fig. 9-13. Balanced seals

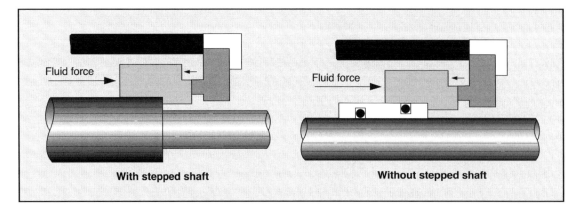

9.46   Sometimes a synthetic rubber bellows is used to seal against leakage between the rotating element and the shaft. This arrangement is shown in Fig. 9-14. Axial movement of the rotating sealing element caused by wear does not affect the position of the shaft-sealing element. Axial movement is compensated for in the bellows portion of the seal.

Special Seals

9.47   Two types of special seals are frequently used on high-pressure boiler feed pumps. Special seals are required because the high rpm and head requirements of the boiler feed pumps would cause other seals to fail in a relatively short time. These special sealing arrangements are shown in Fig. 9-15, on the following page.

9.48   One of the sealing arrangements shown in Fig. 9-15 is called a *packingless seal.* This arrangement does not use a mechanical device to seal the fluid in the pump. Instead, the small clearance between the shaft sleeve and the stuffing box bushing, which is supplied with boiler condensate under pressure, forms the seal. The condensate is injected into the seal area at a pressure approximately 5 to 50 psi above the suction pressure of the pump. A small amount of condensate is drawn into the pump, and the rest is bled off to a drain system.

9.49   The other type of boiler feed pump sealing device in Fig. 9-15 is called the *floating-ring seal.* The floating-ring seal is a mechanical seal.

Fig. 9-14. Bellows shaft-sealing arrangement

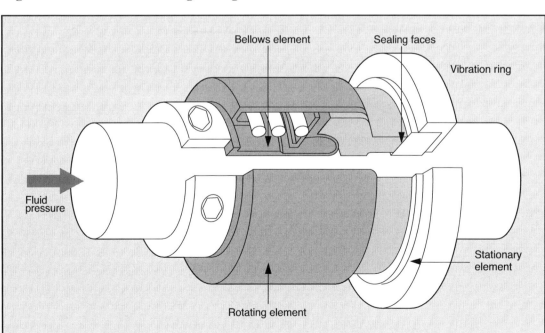

Fig. 9-15. Boiler feed pump seals

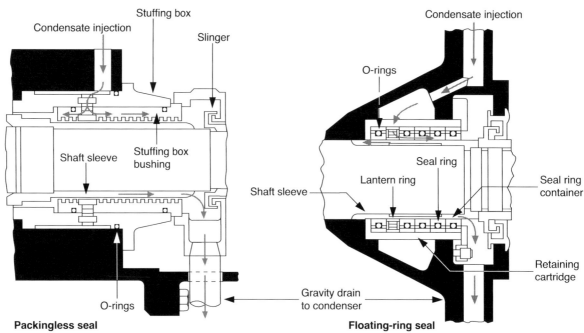

Packingless seal **Floating-ring seal**

Instead of having a single sealing element, however, several seal rings are placed on the shaft sleeve. Each of these rings is supplied with an O-ring. An outer seal-ring container completes the seal. This outer seal-ring container is the stationary part of the seal mechanism. As in the packingless seal application, condensate is injected into the seal at a pressure about 5 to 50 psi above the pump suction pressure.

9.50   Although these two kinds of sealing devices are somewhat unusual in many industries, you should know about them and their operation. You may encounter these or similar seals in high-pressure pump maintenance.

Chapter Ten

Pump Maintenance

10

Pump Bearings

10.01 Many pumps use rotary motion to impart force to the fluid being pumped. The pump impellers are driven by shafts connected to motors or other power sources. The shafts require some means of support and lubrication. To provide support for the shaft, and at the same time reduce the amount of friction between the shaft and pump frame, pumps require bearings and some type of lubrication.

10.02 Nearly all types of bearings have been used on pumps. Bearings in general fall into two major categories—*sliding-contact bearings* and *rolling-contact bearings*. Although sliding-contact bearings, also called *plain* or *sleeve bearings,* were once very popular, they now have been almost entirely replaced by rolling-contact bearings for use on pumps.

Sleeve Bearings

10.03 Because sleeve bearings are seldom used on pumps today, they will be covered only briefly. Sleeve bearings are made of babbitt, bronze, or other soft alloys, depending upon the application and the pump manufacturer. The upper half of a typical sleeve bearing is shown in Fig. 10-1.

10.04 Sleeve bearings have lubrication grooves on their inside surfaces. The grooves store a small amount of lubricant, thus eliminating the need for

Fig. 10-1. Typical sleeve bearing

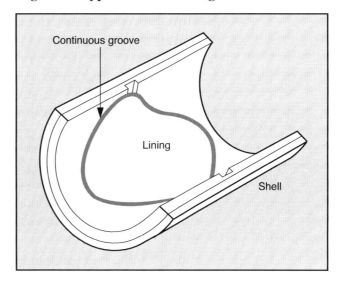

Fig. 10-2. Grooving in a split bearing

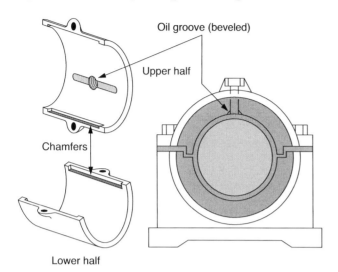

frequent lubrication. Figure 10-2 shows an example of grooving in a split bearing. Only the top half is grooved. Oil is supplied as needed through the oil hole. Notice that the groove — like the continuous groove in the bearing in Fig. 10-1 — does not extend the full length of the bearing surface. If it did, the lubricant could escape.

Antifriction Bearings

10.05   When the surfaces of two objects slide along each other, friction, and thus heat, develop. Antifriction bearings are designed to reduce the friction and heat that develop between the two surfaces. The two types of antifriction bearings are *ball bearings* and *roller bearings*.

10.06   All antifriction bearings consist of four main parts:

- the inner ring

- the outer ring

- the rolling elements (either balls or rollers).

- a cage that keeps the rolling elements evenly spaced.

10.07   Different kinds of bearings are capable of carrying different kinds of loads. Loads parallel to the shaft are called *axial* or *thrust loads.* Loads perpendicular to the shaft are called *radial loads.* Some bearings are designed to carry axial loads, some to carry radial loads, and some a combination of axial and radial loads.

10.08   The four kinds of antifriction bearings used most often to support pump shafts are:

- single-row, deep-groove ball bearing

- angular-contact ball bearing

- spherical roller bearing

- single-row tapered roller bearing.

The four kinds and their operating characteristics are shown in Fig. 10-3.

10.09 Of the four kinds, single-row, deep-groove ball bearings are the most commonly used. They have good radial load capacity and will accept light thrust loading. If the thrust loading becomes heavy, angular-contact bearings can be used. These bearings can be used singly, doubly, or in any combination to support pump shafts.

10.10 Most close-coupled pumps do not have shaft-supporting bearings in the pump housing. Instead, the pump impellers are mounted directly on the motor shaft. In these instances, the motor shaft bearings must absorb the radial and thrust loads from the pump impeller, as well as their own loads. Close-coupled pumps are normally operated by fractional or low-horsepower motors.

10.11 Antifriction bearings used on the majority of pumps must accept at least a small amount of thrust loading. It is important to keep this fact in mind when selecting antifriction bearings. If you anticipate exceptionally high thrust loading, check pump conditions to determine whether or not you need to install thrust bearings.

10.12 The amount of thrust loading present varies with the type of pump. In single-stage, double-suction pumps, the amount of thrust loading is negligible, and a set of double-row ball bearings is sufficient to carry the shaft loads. In multi-stage pumps, spherical roller bearings or a single-row, tapered roller bearing is used on one end of the shaft. A bearing of the same design (facing in the opposite direction) is placed on the other end. The bearings face towards or away from each other, depending on the pump manufacturer. If the

Fig. 10-3. Common antifriction bearings

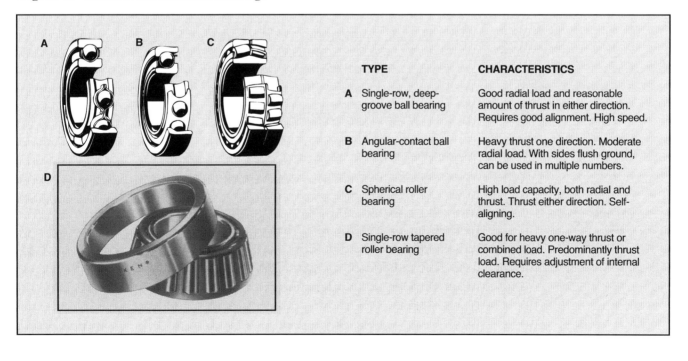

TYPE	CHARACTERISTICS
A Single-row, deep-groove ball bearing	Good radial load and reasonable amount of thrust in either direction. Requires good alignment. High speed.
B Angular-contact ball bearing	Heavy thrust one direction. Moderate radial load. With sides flush ground, can be used in multiple numbers.
C Spherical roller bearing	High load capacity, both radial and thrust. Thrust either direction. Self-aligning.
D Single-row tapered roller bearing	Good for heavy one-way thrust or combined load. Predominantly thrust load. Requires adjustment of internal clearance.

Fig. 10-4. Rubber-lined strut bearing

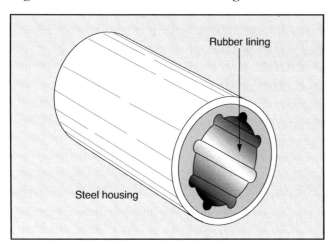

Rubber lining

Steel housing

bearings face in the same direction, they can handle thrust loading in only one direction.

Special Bearings

10.13 Many vertical turbine pumps use a special rubber-lined strut bearing as an intermediate shaft support. As shown in Fig. 10-4, the bearing outer case is made of metal, and the inner bearing surface is made of rubber. The area of contact with the shaft is small, but is sufficient to withstand the load. The bearings are lubricated by the fluid being pumped. Because of their design, these bearings offer excellent resistance to abrasion.

Bearing Lubrication

10.14 Proper lubrication of pump bearings is extremely important. Without proper lubrication, bearings will overheat, rust, corrode, and eventually cause the shaft to seize and stop. If a pump has been shut down for a long period of time without proper lubrication, the bearings can become so rusted that the motor will be unable to turn the pump shaft. Proper lubrication means not only regular lubrication, but use of the proper lubricant in the proper amount. For instance, if a water pump is lubricated with a grease that does not repel water, the water will soon attack the bearings and ruin them.

10.15 In most applications, pump bearings are lubricated with oil or grease. Some special applications use synthetic lubricants. The type of lubricant used depends upon the pump application and the manufacturer's instructions. For example, if the pump is operating outdoors in changing temperatures, oil will work better than grease, because its lubricating qualities are not affected by changing temperatures.

10.16 Oil lubrication is commonly used for light-to-moderate duty in high-speed pumps. When oil is used, check the pump manufacturer's lubrication instructions for the type and viscosity of oil to use. If no lubrication instructions are available, usually a good, filtered, non-detergent mineral oil of grade SAE 10 or 20 can be used. Change the oil at regular, scheduled intervals, or sooner if it becomes dirty or contaminated. Before changing oil, it is a good practice to flush the bearing and the bearing housing or sump with a solvent to make sure that all contaminants and dirt have been removed. This keeps the new oil clean longer.

10.17   There are many ways to ensure proper lubrication of the bearings in a pump. Two methods are shown in Fig. 10-5. Whatever method is used, give it regular attention to make certain that the proper amount of lubricant is reaching the bearings.

10.18   If an oil reservoir or sump is used, overfilling the reservoir can be as serious as not providing enough oil. Overfilling the reservoir will cause the bearings to overheat, as will insufficient lubrication. Some pumping systems for hot fluids have water-cooled lubricating oil sumps or sumps that circulate the oil through a cooler.

10.19   The constant-level oiler shown in Fig. 10-5 is a combination drip-feed and ring-type oiler. The ring used to distribute the oil is the same as in any other ring oiler. The constant-level controlling device, however, does not supply fresh oil all of the time. Its purpose is to maintain a constant oil level in the sump by replacing oil that leaks out.

10.20   Grease is generally used as a lubricant for heavy loads at low to moderate shaft speeds. When grease is used in a pump application, check its grade and consistency to make sure that it is the type specified by the pump manufacturer. Usually, a soda-soap grease with a mineral oil base is acceptable. Bearing grease should be free of clay, mica, talc, and other fillers. These mineral fillers are highly abrasive, even when finely ground and mixed with oil or grease.

Fig. 10-5. Two oil lubricating devices

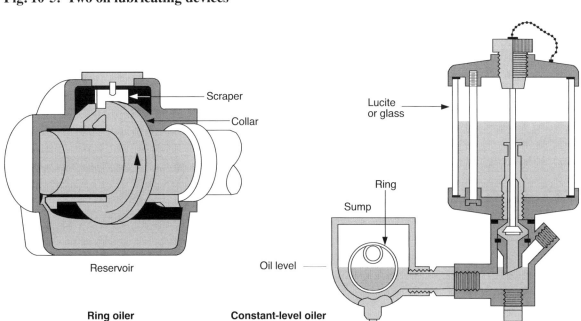

Ring oiler   Constant-level oiler

10.21 Like excessive oiling, excessive greasing of a bearing can cause much damage. In addition to generating heat, an excessive amount of grease can rupture lubricant seals. Ruptured seals can allow contaminants to enter the bearing, thus causing bearing failure.

10.22 Industrial plants normally maintain lubrication schedules for the various pieces of equipment they have installed. This schedule should include pumps. The schedule is based on operating time and load, as well as on pump age and condition. The pump manufacturer might also have recommended lubrication schedules that can be used as guidelines. As a general rule, grease pumps at intervals of approximately three months. If the pump is not often run, greasing intervals can be extended. When the pump is running, inspect the bearings daily for noise, cleanliness, and operating temperature.

10.23 Stand-by pumps and other infrequently used pumps also need attention. Take care to keep moisture out of the bearings. You can do this by wrapping plastic around the bearing and shaft when not in use. Turn the shaft frequently, by hand, to keep the shaft and bearings lubricated. If possible, alternate the operation of stand-by pumps.

10.24 Because a pump has simpler greasing requirements than a large machine tool, for example, pumps do not always have automatic lubrication systems. Some pumps are lubricated with a hand-operated grease gun or by a portable lubrication cart. These carts are usually equipped with an air or electrically operated pump placed in the drum of lubricant. The grease gun is attached to the pump by a long, flexible hose. Many pumps have grease cups, like the one in Fig. 10-6. Turning the cup handle one or two turns at regular intervals supplies the needed lubrication. Be sure to keep the cup filled with the proper lubricant.

Fig. 10-6. Grease cup lubricators

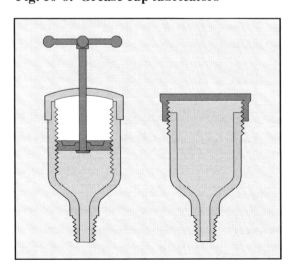

Bearing Seals

10.25 Bearing seals come in an almost endless variety. This chapter describes some of the more common contact-type seals used with pump bearings. *Contact seals* retain lubricant and exclude dirt and other contaminants by maintaining a constant sealing contact between the seal lip and the rotating shaft or sleeve.

10.26 The bearing seal shown on the left in Fig. 10-7 is positioned so that its sealing lip faces the fluid it retains. The seal on the right in Fig. 10-7 is a felt seal with an oil slinger placed on the

Fig. 10-7. Bearing lubricant seals

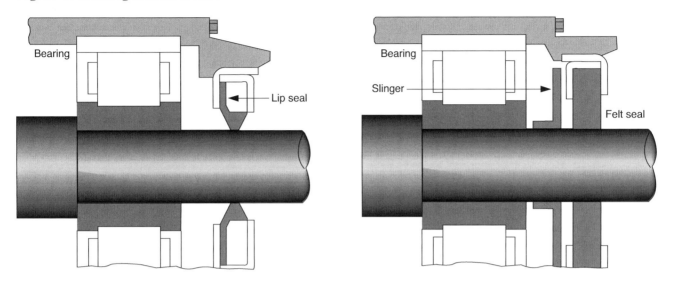

fluid side to keep the oil away from the seal. These seals are different from the sealing devices (stuffing boxes and mechanical seals) used to seal fluids within the pump. Design varies with the amount of lubricant each seal must retain.

10.27   Although the seals shown in Fig. 10-7 have only one sealing lip, some seals have two or more. The number of seal lips and the material from which they are made depend upon the degree of sealing required. Seals are commonly made from leather, felt, and synthetic compounds.

10.28   Felt seals are used for slow shaft speed applications in which only small amounts of lubricant are present. Leather seals are also used for slow-speed applications, but they are usually used to retain large amounts of lubricant. They can tolerate a slightly rough or irregular shaft surface without wearing out quickly. Synthetic seals are used for high-speed applications and large lubricant quantities. These seals require ground or polished shaft surfaces.

10.29   Synthetic seals are usually made from rubber compounds, nitriles, polyacrylates, and silicones. Frequently, bearings on similar pumps will have different seals. If you have to change seals, be sure that the replacement seal is either the same as the existing seal, or a recommended substitute. In many cases, you can use seals of different manufacturers interchangeably if the seal material is the same. In an emergency, you can usually use seals of different materials, although seal life might be shortened.

10.30   If bearing seal failure is a recurring problem on a particular pump, inspect the shaft. If the shaft is rough or corroded, you will need to recondition it or install a new shaft or shaft sleeve before installing new seals. In some cases, the shaft might have to be built up before it can be reconditioned.

Pump Installation

10.31   There are three steps in pump installation:

- base installation

- pump alignment

- piping connection.

All of these steps are essential to proper pump operation and should not be done hastily or poorly. In some instances, pumps are installed by outside contractors during plant construction. In many cases, however, a plant's maintenance department is responsible for installing new pumps. Most manufacturers recommend that certain procedures be followed. This chapter outlines some of the common procedures.

10.32   Large pumps are usually installed on concrete pads, as shown in Fig. 10-8. Anchor bolts in the pad keep the pump base rigid and dampen vibration, which helps reduce piping leaks. The first step in installing a large pump is to excavate the floor to accommodate the pad, as specified by the plant engineer or pump manufacturer.

10.33   Next, build a wooden form that will allow the pad to extend 8 to 12 in. above the floor. Then, build a wooden frame and drill it to match the bolt-hole pattern of the pump base. Place the frame over the form to hold the anchor bolts in position. The bolt threads must extend far enough above the concrete pad to pass through the pump base and still leave room

Fig. 10-8. Methods of checking shaft alignment

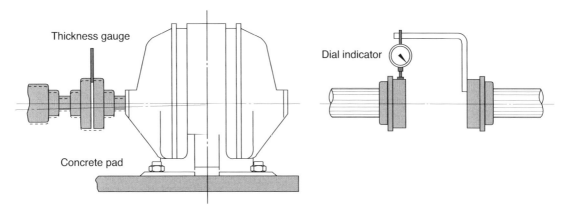

for nuts and washers. Fasten the bolts to the frame with nuts and pour the concrete.

10.34   After the concrete has cured, remove the form and place the pump base in position on the pad. Using a mechanic's level, level the base in both directions. Place shims or wedges wherever needed to keep the base level. Then tighten the anchor bolt nuts to secure the base. Fill in any irregular areas beneath the edges of the base with grout and allow it to cure.

10.35   After the base is firmly in place and the grout has cured, place the pump and motor on the base. If they are separate pieces, make sure they are properly aligned. Use thickness gauges or a dial indicator, as shown in Fig. 10-8, to check for proper alignment at the coupling. If necessary, add shims beneath the pump or motor to correct misalignment.

10.36   After the pump and motor are aligned and bolted down, connect the piping. Correct piping installation is most important on the suction side of the pump. If piping is improperly installed on the suction side, air pockets can form. These air pockets have a detrimental effect on the pump's operation and can cause maintenance problems. Also, make sure the piping is not being supported by the pump housing. Stress on the pump housing should be avoided. Correct and incorrect installation techniques for the pump suction piping are shown in Fig. 10-9, on the following page.

Pump Maintenance

10.37   Although many pump maintenance procedures vary with the kind of pump, many other procedures are the same on all pumps. For example, pump bearings and sealing devices operate in a similar manner, regardless of the pump on which they are installed. Bearing maintenance usually involves only periodic lubrication. Stuffing boxes require only minor adjustments from time to time, and mechanical seals require only a visual inspection for leakage. The only seals that require special attention are those used on chemical or difficult-material pumps.

10.38   Pumps have a tendency to overheat if used in an environment that is too hot, and freeze if the environment gets too cold. If the pump is located outdoors or in an unusual place (near a furnace or chilling compartment, for example), consider providing protection for the pump. Specially designed casings and insulation are available for this purpose.

10.39   The following maintenance tips cover some of the most common pump problems. Problems are grouped according to pump type. Table 10-1, on page 129, describes several common pump problems, identifies their symptoms and causes, and lists likely steps toward their solutions.

Fig. 10-9. Suction pipe installation

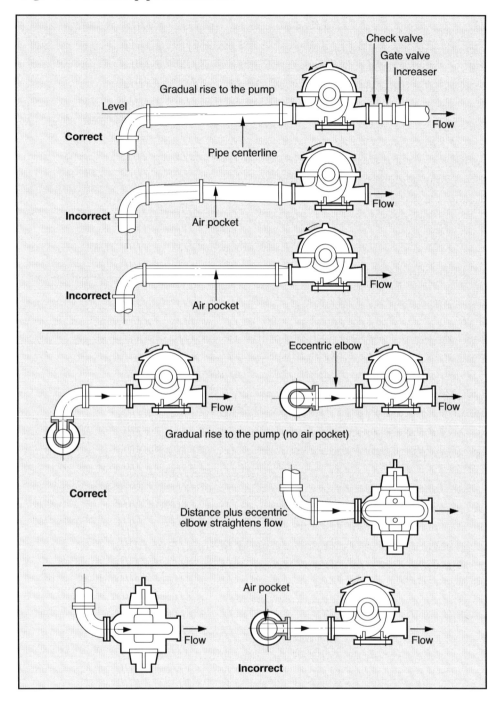

End-Suction Centrifugal Pumps

10.40   End-suction centrifugal pump maintenance problems are generally confined to only a few components. These components are the casings, wearing rings, and impellers. Pump casings cause problems when the fluid handled by the pump is corrosive or incompatible with the pump. Pump casings used with corrosive fluids are usually designed to resist the

Table 10-1. Pump problems

Symptom and cause	Solution
NO LIQUID DELIVERED Lack of prime. Suction lift too high. Discharge head too high. Impeller plugged.	Fill pump and suction pipe completely with liquid. If no obstruction at inlet, check for pipe friction losses. If static lift is too high, liquid to be pumped must be raised or pump lowered. Check pipe friction losses. Check that valves are wide open. Dismantle pump and clean impeller.
NOT ENOUGH LIQUID DELIVERED Air leaks in suction piping. Air leaks in stuffing box. Impeller partially plugged. Defective impeller. Defective packing or seal. Suction not immersed enough.	Test flanges for leakage. Suction line can be tested by plugging inlet and putting line under pressure. Increase seal liquid pressure to above atmosphere. Dismantle pump and clean impeller. Inspect impeller and shaft. Replace if damaged or vane sections badly eroded. Replace packing or mechanical seal. Lower inlet.
NOT ENOUGH PRESSURE Speed too low. Air leaks in suction piping. Mechanical defects. Obstruction in liquid passages. Air or gas bubbles in liquid.	Check whether motor is receiving full voltage. Test flanges for leakage. Suction line can be tested by plugging inlet and putting line under pressure. Inspect impeller and shaft. Replace if damaged or vane sections badly eroded. Replace packing or mechanical seal. Dismantle pump, inspect passages, and remove obstruction. Possibility of overrated pump. Periodically exhaust accumulated air.
PUMP OPERATES FOR SHORT TIME THEN STOPS Incomplete priming. Air leaks in suction piping. Air leaks in stuffing box.	Free pump, piping, and valves of all air. Correct any high points in suction line. Test flanges for leakage. Suction line can be tested by plugging inlet and putting line under pressure. Increase seal liquid pressure to above atmosphere.
PUMP TAKES TOO MUCH POWER Mechanical defects. Suction not immersed enough. Stuffing box too tight. Shaft bent or damaged. Failure of pump parts	Inspect impeller and shaft. Replace if damaged or vane sections badly eroded. Replace packing or mechanical seal. Lower inlet. Release gland pressure. Check deflection of rotor by turning on bearing journals. Check bearings and impeller for damage.

corrosive action of the fluid. If only a small amount of corrosive fluid is suspended in the fluid being pumped, however, the effect on the pump is small. Most pump casings are of such size and strength that slight corrosion of the interior will not affect pumping capacity. In some cases, casings that corrode through completely can be patched without any decrease in pump capacity.

10.41 The impeller is the heart of an end-suction centrifugal pump. If an impeller is seriously damaged by corrosion or abrasion, the pump's overall capacity will be reduced. Capacity is also reduced when the impeller becomes clogged or has excessive material buildup. Selection of the proper impeller shape and the proper impeller material for the fluid being pumped is essential to good impeller performance.

10.42 The wearing rings in an end-suction centrifugal pump are the components that most often require maintenance. Although many small centrifugal pumps have no wearing rings, most larger pumps do. Wearing rings maintain a minimum clearance between the impeller and the casing. They can be installed on both the housing and the impeller. Minimum impeller clearance improves pump capacity.

10.43 In order to extend their operating life and reduce replacement costs, many impeller wearing rings are adjustable. Once adjusted, locknuts hold them in place. The type and amount of impurities suspended in the fluid being pumped determines the rate at which wearing rings wear.

10.44 If the pumped fluid has a high chemical content, the chemical can attack the wearing rings and corrode them quickly. This condition can be improved by selecting the proper wearing ring material. In some cases, short wearing-ring life is acceptable because corrosion of the wearing rings protects the pump casing and impeller from chemical attack.

Vertical Turbine Pumps

10.45 Vertical turbine pump maintenance problems are similar to those of other centrifugal pumps. Bowl and impeller corrosion, impeller clogging, obstructions, and blinding of the suction bell will prevent the pump from pumping its required capacity. Although the pump suction may be below the fluid it is pumping, the suction bell can still become clogged with debris.

10.46 Vertical turbine pumps differ from end-suction centrifugal pumps in the way in which the impeller clearances are adjusted. Most vertical turbine pumps do not have wearing rings. Impeller clearance is changed by adjusting the drive shaft at the motor, as shown in Fig. 10-10. If the pump is multistage, all impellers are adjusted at the same time and by the same amount.

Fig. 10-10. Shaft adjustment in a vertical turbine pump

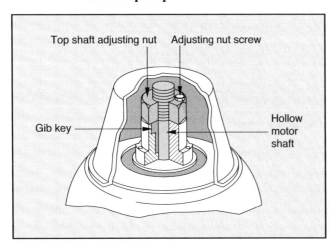

Rotary Pumps

10.47 Unlike the impellers of end-suction centrifugal or turbine pumps, the impellers of most rotary pumps are subject to very little wear by abrasive materials. The major maintenance problems in these pumps occur in the bearings and seals. This statement is especially true when the bearing is lubricated by the fluid being pumped. To extend bearing life, maintain proper alignment between the end caps and the pump casing during pump assembly.

10.48 Impeller wear by abrasive materials is greatest in screw and vane pumps where there is only a small amount of clearance between the rotors or impellers and the pump casing. Internal gear pump impellers are also subject to wear by abrasives because of the close clearances between the mating teeth. Most tooth wear is caused by the abrasive nature of the material, not by tooth contact. Keeping pumps as clean as possible helps eliminate this type of wear.

Reciprocating Pumps

10.49 Maintenance problems in reciprocating pumps usually involve the stuffing boxes or seals at the connecting rod and the piston rings. Because of the constant reversing motion and fluctuating pressures within the pump, the piston rings in the fluid section generally wear out sooner than any other component in the pump.

10.50 Lack of fluid pressure while the pump is running often indicates worn piston rings. Pump pressure might also be low if any of the internal check valves are stuck open. Always check the pump valves before you replace piston rings. In addition, a leaking stuffing box at the end of the connecting rod might cause the pump to act as if it had worn piston rings.

10.51 In high-pressure pumps, the condition of the connecting rod stuffing boxes is critical. They must be kept in good condition at all times. Loss of pressure through the stuffing box of a high-pressure pump can cause serious damage or personal injury if neglected.

Difficult-Material Pumps

10.52 Difficult-material pumps are usually made in the standard pump types already discussed. Because they resemble standard pumps, always check for the typical maintenance problems of the specific pump type first.

10.53 Many maintenance problems in difficult-material pumps are caused by the material itself. Abrasive fluids, slurries, trash, high-viscosity materials, and chemicals all cause their own unique problems. Check with the pump manufacturer for maintenance information related to specific applications.

Other Maintenance Problems

10.54 Not all pumping system problems are caused by the pump. Frequently, obstructions in the suction or discharge piping reduce the pump capacity and cause the pump to act as though it were operating improperly. If the pump does not produce its required capacity, first check suction screens for blinding. In addition, improper valve installation (such as reversed check valves) can cause serious operation problems for the pump.

Contributions from the following sources are appreciated:

Figure 3-2.	Worthington Division, McGraw-Edison Company
Figure 3-3.	Price Pump Co., Worthington Division, McGraw-Edison Company
Figure 4-1.	Peerless Pump
	Burks Pumps
Figure 4-2.	Byron Jackson Pumps
Figure 4-5.	Byron Jackson Pumps
Figure 4-6.	Lawrence Pumps, Inc.
Figure 4-8.	Peerless Pump
Figure 4-9.	Lawrence Pumps, Inc.
Figure 5-2.	Viking Pumps
Figure 5-3.	Worthington Division, McGraw-Edison Company
Figure 5-4.	Viking Pump Division, Houdaille Industries, Inc.
Figure 5-7.	Roper Pump Company
Figure 5-9.	IMO Pump Division of Transamerica Delaval, Inc.
Figure 5-10.	Blackmer Pump Div./Dover Corp.
Figure 5-11.	Hypro, A Division of Lear Siegler, Inc.
Figure 5-15.	ITT Jabsco Products
Figure 6-1.	Binks Manufacturing Company, Union Pump Company
Figure 6-4.	Worthington Division, McGraw-Edison Company
Figure 6-6.	Worthington Division, McGraw-Edison Company
Figure 6-8.	Worthington Division, McGraw-Edison Company
Figure 6-9.	Worthington Division, McGraw-Edison Company
Figure 6-10.	Binks Manufacturing Company, Grover Manufacturing Corp.
Figure 6-12.	Binks Manufacturing Company
Figure 7-1.	Jaeco Pump Company
Figure 7-2.	Viking Pump Division, Houdaille Industries, Inc.
Figure 7-4.	Lubriquip Div., Houdaille Industries, Inc.
Figure 7-6.	The Madden Corp.
Figure 7-7.	BIF, A Unit of General Signal
Figure 7-8.	Jaeco Pump Company
Figure 7-11.	Blackmer Pump Div./Dover Corp.
Figure 8-4.	Vanton Pump & Equipment Co.
Figure 8-5.	Moyno Products, Fluids Handling Division, Robbins & Meyers, Inc.
Figure 8-6.	SERFILCO, Ltd
Figure 8-11.	PACO Pump Company
Figure 8-12.	The Gorman-Rupp Co.
Figure 8-14.	The Warren Rupp Company
Figure 8-15.	Wagener Pump Division, Detroit Stoker Company
Figure 8-16.	The Gorman-Rupp Co.
Figure 9-9.	Garlock Mechanical Packing Division
Figure 9-14.	Garlock Mechanical Packing Division
Figure 10-3.	The Timken Company
Figure 10-9.	Allis-Chalmers/Fluid Products Company